Bonne Chance!

— Listening & Oral for Leaving Cert French —

Elizabeth Hayes-Lyne

Serena Butler

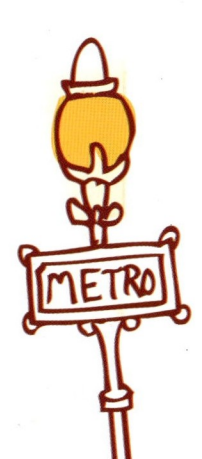

Gill & Macmillan

Gill & Macmillan
Hume Avenue
Park West
Dublin 12
www.gillmacmillan.ie

© Elizabeth Hayes-Lyne 2014
978 07171 5960 4

Design and print origination by Design Image

The paper used in this book is made from the wood pulp of managed forests. For every tree felled, at least one tree is planted, thereby renewing natural resources.

All rights reserved. No part of this publication may be copied, reproduced or transmitted in any form or by any means without written permission of the publishers or else under the terms of any licence permitting limited copying issued by the Irish Copyright Licensing Agency.

Any links to external websites should not be construed as an endorsement by Gill & Macmillan of the content or view of the linked material. Furthermore it cannot be guaranteed that all external links will be live.

For permission to reproduce photographs, the author and publisher gratefully acknowledge the following:

© Alamy: 33, 41, 47, 48, 84, 112, 124, 126, 127, 138, 143; © Photocall Ireland: 46, 49, 59B, 97, 100; © Shutterstock: 1, 19, 21, 24, 33, 35, 62, 73, 87, 98, 101, 110T, 110B, 114, 125, 139, 141; © Shutterstock/Jaggat Rashidi: 59T, 61; © Shutterstock/Paul Prescott: 72; © Shutterstock/pio3: 71, 75.

The author and publisher have made every effort to trace all copyright holders, but if any has been inadvertently overlooked we would be pleased to make the necessary arrangement at the first opportunity.

Contents

Introduction 1

Chapitre 1 La famille 19
Aural Section 19
- A Je vous présente ma famille 19
- B Les disputes en famille 20
- C Les parents stricts 20
- D Les familles monoparentales 21
- E L'échange des bébés à la naissance 21
- F Les allocations familiales 22
- G Le conflit entre générations 23
- H Leaving Cert 2012 Section II 23
- I Les faits divers 24

Oral Section – *Let's Get Talking* 25

Chapitre 2 Les amis et l'amitié 33
Aural Section 33
- A Décrivez votre meilleur ami 33
- B L'amitié est sacrée 34
- C La pression des pairs 34
- D Quels sont vos passe-temps ? 35
- E La mode et le bal des débutantes 36
- F Les sorties 36
- G 1996 Leaving Cert, Section III 37
- H Les faits divers 37

Oral Section – *Let's Get Talking* 38

Chapitre 3 La maison et le quartier 46
Aural Section 46
- A Comment est votre maison ? 46
- B Les sans abris 46
- C Les quartiers chauds de Paris et les émeutes 47
- D Des maisons détruites en Chine 48
- E Les maisons écologiques 48
- F Les lotissements fantômes 49
- G Leaving Cert Section III 2010 49
- H Leaving Cert Section I 2011 50
- I Les faits divers 50

Oral Section – *Let's Get Talking* 51

Chapitre 4 Le sport 59
Aural Section 59
- A Les Jeux Olympiques 59
- B Le sport sanguinaire 60
- C L'imparitalité des arbîtres 60
- D Les sportifs – sont-ils trop payés ? 61
- E Le sport et la publicité d'alcool 61
- F Pourquoi les sportifs se dopent-ils ? 62
- G Leaving Cert 1998 Section 1 63
- H Les faits divers 63

Oral Section – *Let's Get Talking* 64

Chapitre 5 L'économie 71
Aural Section 71
- A Les petits boulots 71
- B Le tigre celtique ! 72
- C La main d'œuvre enfantine 72
- D La chute bancaire 73
- E Le chômage 74
- F Les compagnies aériennes à bas prix 74
- G Leaving Cert 2011 Section II 75
- H Les faits divers 76

Oral Section – *Let's Get Talking* 76

Chapitre 6 L'école 84
Aural Section 84
- A Les régles de l'école 84
- B Le vandalisme dans les écoles et leurs environs 85
- C Le système de points 85
- D Le harcèlement à l'école 86
- E Est-ce que les diplômes sont nécessaires pour réussir dans la vie ? 87
- F Pour ou contre l'uniforme scolaire 87
- G Les écoles mixtes contre les écoles non-mixtes 88
- H Leaving Cert 2012 Section III 88
- I Les faits divers 89

Oral Section – *Let's Get Talking* 90

Chapitre 7 L'environnement — 97
Aural Section — 97
- A Pourquoi payer l'eau — 97
- B Les forêts tropicales — 98
- C L'énergie solaire — 98
- D Les déchets nucléaires — 99
- E Le recyclage — 99
- F Les inondations — 100
- G Leaving Cert 2003 Section 1 — 100
- H L'empreinte écologique — 101
- I Les faits divers — 101

Oral Section – *Let's Get Talking* — 102

Chapitre 8 La santé — 110
Aural Section — 110
- A La nourriture de mauvaise qualité — 110
- B Des risques de santé pour les jeunes — 111
- C Le cancer — 111
- D L'obésité — 112
- E L'anorexie — 113
- F Les organismes génétiquement modifiés — 113
- G Leaving Cert 2001 Section II — 114
- H Les faits divers — 115

Oral Section – *Let's Get Talking* — 116

Chapitre 9 La technologie — 124
Aural Section — 124
- A La technologie moderne — 124
- B La nano-technologie — 125
- C Les portables — 125
- D L'internet — 126
- E La télévision — 127
- F Le commerce en ligne — 127
- G Leaving Cert Ordinary Level 2009 Section 1 — 128
- H Les faits divers — 129

Oral Section – *Let's Get Talking* — 129

Chapitre 10 Les problèmes sociaux — 138
Aural Section — 138
- A La pauvreté, la drogue et l'émigration — 138
- B Le jeu de hasard — 139
- C La discrimination raciale — 139
- D Les mannequins de taille zéro — 140
- E La peine de mort — 141
- F Le cyber-harcèlement — 141
- G Les célébrités — 142
- H La puissance de la publicité — 142
- I Le clonage — 143
- J L'expérimentation animale — 144

Oral Section – *Let's Get Talking* — 145

Introduction

About this book

Bonne Chance! is an exciting new book which will help you reach your highest potential in French. *Bonne Chance!* is not just a book, it is a complete package for the aural and oral components of the Leaving Certificate French examination.

Rather than claiming to be an exhaustive solution to your French needs, *Bonne Chance!* is the *definitive* guide to the Leaving Cert Aural and Oral components of the exam. The rationale behind *Bonne Chance!* is simple: language learning is like a puzzle. You have grammar on one side and words on the other. The trick is to put the pieces together in order to make correct sentences. It is outside the remit of this book to include a grammar section but if you follow the examples of the key constructions and the vocabulary, you too will soon be writing flawless French. I disagree with learning paragraphs on various topics off by heart, as the exam itself is so unpredictable. It is a far better idea to learn how to write correctly, and develop a store of sayings which, when used appropriately, will enrich your language. Vocabulary is the key to any language, as without words conversation would be impossible. *Bonne Chance!* provides you with the *tools* necessary to succeed. In order to reach your highest potential in French, you must experiment with words and try to make sentences which will show your mastery over the language.

Having worked as a secondary teacher for the last 10 years in Ireland, and previously having worked in France for 10 years, I'm happy to say that my results speak for themselves; over 40% of my students attain an A grade in the Leaving Certificate. Now you can use the *Bonne Chance!* method for consistently excellent results.

Traditional phonetics are really only understood by linguists, but *Bonne Chance!* simplifies phonetics so they are easily understood by students, allowing them to become confident in expressing themselves correctly in French and, as a result, the aural component becomes easy. I would like to wish all of you *Bonne Chance!* in your French studies.

Bon courage à vous tous.
Elizabeth Hayes-Lyne

Structure of each chapter

Each chapter follows the same structure, the key elements of which are explained below:

Aural Section

Each aural exercise begins with *Le vocabulaire clé* or the **key vocabulary** needed to understand the listening piece which follows. I suggest that you begin by familiarising yourself with the *vocabulaire clé* and then play the listening piece.

There are an average of 7 listening pieces per chapter. Each chapter is based on a specific topic, and the vocabulary and listening pieces all address a particular facet of this topic. Among the myriad of topics available to me, I have chosen to go with the **ten most popular topics that appear on the Leaving Cert French Papers**. I have studied the exam papers from as far back as the 80s and have chosen topics which I feel will be the most beneficial for you to focus on.

| Student Level 1 | Student Level 2 | Student Level 3 | Teacher Level 1 | Teacher Level 2 | Teacher Level 3 |

Each listening piece in *Bonne Chance!* has been meticulously researched and written with the capabilities of the different students in mind. There are **three levels of listening** throughout the book. Level one is for students who find French particularly challenging. It is also an excellent way of easing transition or 5th year students into the aural component of the Leaving Certificate. Level two is a little more difficult, but is still very accessible to students, and would be excellent for mixed-ability classes. The listening pieces classed as level three are quite difficult, but again, if the students learn how to pronounce all the words on the topic in question, these listening pieces are very well worth attempting. Students will be surprised how much they will have learnt by the time they reach a level three piece.

The Oral Section – Let's Get Talking

There are many French books on the market which give students an abundance of choice and cover every possible situation for this section. I have been preparing students for the oral component of the exam for many years, and it is my contention that students try to learn too much! Remember that the oral exam is a **conversation** between the student and highly trained professionals. The examiner will not expect a student to be completely fluent. The aim of the oral is for a student to reach enough proficiency not to be lost in a French setting. *Bonne Chance!* gives students a total of 100 questions. There are **ten questions based on each topic**, with easily understood phonetics. A lot of students feel powerless to practice the oral, but with *Bonne Chance!* they have the possibility of practising typical questions and answers with a friend or family member. Most students know what to say but sometimes they do not understand the question. *Bonne Chance!* takes the worry out of this, as a lot of typical questions are dealt with. I have then given a sample answer, which the student should use as a guide and personalise for themselves.

Ten common questions
As a typical oral examination lasts between 12-15 minutes, I have decided to only include the absolute essential questions that a student should familiarise themselves with. In each chapter, the student is presented with 10 questions, any of which they may reasonably expect to be asked.

Dix questions et réponses possibles
Here the 10 questions which have been presented to the students are answered with a possible response. The aim of this strategy is two-fold. Firstly it gives the students an idea of what questions to expect, and secondly, it exposes the student to possible answers. You will also notice that in this section, as with the 10 common questions, the material is presented phonetically. This is done in order that students can study alone, or with a friend or family member, without that.

Le vocabulaire essentiel
Bonne Chance! contains well in excess of **1000 words of vocabulary**. There are over 100 words of vocabulary per chapter. 1000 words may seem like a lot, but the average person uses between 800 and 1200 words a day! Students should learn a few words every day, and incorporate them into their writing. The more words that students are exposed to, the greater chance they will have to understand the reading comprehensions. I have added the phonetics to the vocabulary here also, as a lot of these words tend to come up in the aural section of the Leaving Certificate.

Dix constructions clés
I could have just given students a mixture of written paragraphs, and said 'work away, learn these'. However, my philosophy is not to give students a fish every day, but to give them the fishing rod, and teach them how to fish for themselves. In *Bonne Chance!* there are **100 key constructions**, which are used to enrich your writing and reading skills. I have given you a sample sentence with each construction and would suggest that students take the construction, use some of their new *vocabulaire essentiel*, and put sentences together. This will **give students a level of mastery** over the language, and promote autonomous learning. I also find that these are fantastic exercises to reinforce the learning of a topic.

Dix expressions authentiques et ludiques
Bonne Chance! contains **100 native French phrases/expressions**.
   The Written Expression or *La Production Écrite* is very important for the Leaving Cert. I would strongly advise that you use these sayings to enrich your written expression, but do get your teacher to read over your work, to make sure that you are using them in a correct and coherent manner.

Higher Level Leaving Cert Exam Paper

The French Higher Level examination comprises three components – Written, Aural and Oral. The Written paper consists of two sections – Reading Comprehension and Written Expression.

You have two and a half hours to complete the reading and written part of the French paper, for a total of 220 marks.
- Written – 220 marks
- Oral – 100 marks
- Aural – 80 marks

Written Examination

Section I – Compréhension Écrite (120 marks)

This section carries 120 marks in the form of two reading comprehensions, worth 60 marks each.
- Question 1: Journalistic Passage
- Question 2: Literary Passage

You must answer both questions.

Each of Questions 1 and 2 contain ten segments to be answered in French, followed by one segment to be answered in Irish or English.

There is no excuse not to have enough reading material for the exam. Read all your past exam papers and every single reading comprehension from your text book. Log on to www.google.fr and google an article every few days, just to get more practice in. I strongly advise against using google translate as it translates literally and does not take context into consideration. www.wordreference.com is an excellent translation site. This site will only translate one word at a time, so it can be frustrating but there are interesting forums to help you within the site. Familiarise yourself with the way in which questions are asked at the end of each reading comprehension.

Section II – Production Écrite (100 marks)

Students are asked to answer Question 1 and two questions from Questions 2, 3 and 4. All questions to be answered in French.
- **Question 1** is compulsory (90 words approximately). It is worth 40 marks and is linked in some way to the two reading comprehensions. You are given an (a) or (b) choice. One is usually a reflective piece of writing, which will require a good working knowledge of the imperfect (*imparfait*) and compound past (*passé composé*). The other piece is generally more topical.
- Then you **choose two** more questions from **questions 2 to 4** (75 words approximately). These are worth 30 marks each. Within each question, you must decide between (a) and (b). Question 2 will usually contain a diary entry and/or a letter or e-mail. Questions 3 and 4 are usually comprised of topical issues.

Chief Examiner's Notes on Written Work

Those who performed really well at the written production addressed the issues set out in the tasks and developed them in idiomatic and accurate French. Others, however, relied heavily on learnt-off material without adapting it to the particular demands of the chosen task. Some candidates seem to have learnt by heart generic introductory and closing paragraphs and stock phrases which they felt would suit all topics. In such cases, however, the communicative intention was often stultified as – once the lengthy introduction and conclusion were read – the content relating to the stimulus itself was sparse. Other candidates, who resorted to clichés and proverbs, were unable to mask their lack of real language skills. Examiners commented that the standard of written French was generally high, and that candidates appeared to find the range of topics on offer attractive and stimulating. However, the gap between those who performed really well and those who performed very poorly was once again marked. Specifically, examiners cited poor performance at basic sentence construction, use of tenses, agreements, accents and negatives. A small number of candidates answered more questions than was required. This was generally of no benefit to them; in many cases, the decision to do an extra question was to the detriment of the three primary questions where mistakes were made which may have been avoided had candidates not been so rushed. Similarly, many candidates who wrote answers out fully in pencil as rough-work, and then painstakingly re-wrote the entire answers again in pen on their answer-book, wasted much time that it would have been more worthwhile to spend refining and perfecting their work.

Students perform best when they write in a personal, spontaneous and natural way. It is important that students recognise the meanings of the specific questions such as *trouvez, citez, relevez, un mot, une expression, une phrase, un élément*, etc, as penalties incurred in the Reading Comprehension would be greatly reduced by this knowledge. *Bonne Chance!* gives students the two main elements needed to write French correctly: vocabulary and grammatical constructions. Students should take the time to construct their own sentences to gain mastery over the language.

Top Tips for the Written Exam:

1. Read as much as possible!
2. Explore various meanings within a text.
3. Constantly revise grammar, including the main verb tenses, agreement of adjectives, plurals, negative and interrogative forms, and prepositions.
4. Recognise grammatical elements within a sentence, adverbs, adjectives, pronouns etc.
5. Practise simple, grammatically accurate sentences.
6. Write in a personal, authentic manner.
7. *Bonne Chance!* contains over 100 aural pieces, and students should look at the list of topics in the Contents page, look up the vocabulary section, and start writing their own paragraphs of approximately 100 words.
8. Do not learn big long essays off by heart on every topic. You will get bogged down and become disheartened. Write three points on each topic and learn about twenty words of vocabulary.
9. Have decent sentences to begin and end a written piece.
10. Use accurate grammatical constructions, and use your verbs correctly.
11. Rule of Agreement.

Oral Examination

	Pronunciation	Structure	Communication	Vocabulary
HIGHER 25%	20 marks	30 marks	30 marks	20 marks
ORDINARY 20%	20 marks	30 marks	30 marks	20 marks

Introduction

The oral component accounts for 25% of marks at Higher Level and 20% of marks at Ordinary Level. The oral examination is conducted in the same way for both Higher and Ordinary Level candidates. All students are marked out of a total of 100 and the marks of Ordinary Level candidates are adjusted at a later stage.

The format of the oral examination consists of a conversation of approximately twelve minutes' duration during which students are given the opportunity to display their proficiency in the spoken language. Students have the option of bringing in a document of their choice. This could consist of a photograph or picture, a newspaper or magazine article, a literary text or a project. All candidates are marked out of a total of **100** marks, which are allocated as follows:
- Pronunciation 20 marks
- Vocabulary 20 marks
- Structure 30 marks
- Communication 30 marks.

(i) Pronunciation

'For many candidates, pronunciation is the aspect of language most in need of attention.' Chief Examiner's Report, 2010

If you really want to do well in the oral exam, you must refine your French accent. It doesn't matter if it sounds strange to you. To an examiner, it will ensure you achieve top marks in this section. Remember the following:
- Do not pronounce the –ent at the end of a verb. i.e.: *ils mangent* is pronounced eel monge.
- The 'h' in French is silent e.g.: *hôpital* is pronounced op-pi-tal.
- The 'ch' is pronounced like 'sh' for example *chimie* = shim-mee.
- All qu is pronounced K as in *Que* = kuh.

The Chief Examiner's Report of 2010 makes the point that pronunciation was all too often the *weakest element* in a candidate's performance. Many candidates failed entirely to suppress their local accent. Others pronounced their opening sentences well but then floundered. Examiners frequently refer to learnt-off material as being **seriously detrimental to good pronunciation**. Candidates may not realise that it is not sufficient to have learnt by heart an impressive amount of material if their inability to pronounce French reasonably correctly renders their presentation almost unintelligible. With *Bonne Chance!* students are given 100 typical questions to practise, with easy to understand phonetics. With these phonetics, students can practise at school, or at home, or even on their own. I have taken the Chief Examiner's report which highlights problem areas with pronunciation and written in how to pronounce the words correctly. The following problem areas were identified:

1. Pronouncing final silent consonant, e.g. *trucs* = trook, *trop* = tro, *cours* = coor, *sport* = spor, *heures* = er, *je sors* = je sor
2. Mispronunciation of words such as: *natation, installation, récréation, émission*: *natation* = na-tass-yon, *installation* = an-stal-lass-yon, *récréation* = reh-cray-ass-yon, *émission* = ay-miss-yon
3. Difficulty in pronouncing correctly the 'gn' in *gagner* = gan-yay, *campagne* = cam-pan; *Espagne* = Ess-pan
4. Confusion between *ville* = veel, *mille* = meel, *tranquille* = tron-keel as opposed to *famille* = fam-mee, *fille* = fee, *pavillon* = pav-vee-on
5. Difficulty with the nasal sounds in words, e.g. *examen* = egg-za-mahn; *jardin* = jar-dahn; *vin* = vahn, *mon* = mohn
6. Little or no effort to pronounce the French 'r'
7. Failure to observe the silent 'e' or 'ent' in the Present Tense, e.g. *je joue* = je joo, *il aime* = il em, *elles regardent* = elle re-gard
8. Confusion of *matière* = mat-tee-air/ *métier* = met-tee-ay, *vie* = vee / *ville* = veel, *aîné* = en-nay / *année* = an-nay, *cheveux* = che-veuh/ *chevaux* = che-voh
9. Final é in the *Passé Composé* should be pronounced as 'ay' but was left silent, e.g. *j'ai joué* pronounced *j'ai joue*
10. Not making correct liaison, e.g. *les élèves* (anytime you have an 's' followed by a vowel in French, you pull the words together). The above example should be pronounced 'lays-el-lev = les élèves'
11. Mispronunciation of school subjects, especially *le français, la chimie, la biologie*: *le français* = le fron-say, *la chimie* = la shim-mee, *la biologie* = la bee-ol-oh-jee
12. Mispronunciation of common nouns such as *parents, poulet, sœur, travaille*: *parents* = par-ron, *poulet* = poo-lay, *sœur* = seur, *travaille* = tra-vye
13. No distinction between the pronunciation of *un* and *une*: *un* = an and *une* = oone

(ii) Vocabulary

Look at the following topics and decide whether or not you have the requisite vocabulary.
- *ma famille, moi-même, ma maison, mon quartier*
- *mon école, mes amis et ma routine*
- *mes loisirs et le weekend*
- *ce que je veux faire à l'avenir, mes études, ma carrière*
- *mes vacances et mes voyages*
- *l'été dernier, le weekend dernier*
- *l'année prochaine, l'été prochain*
- *le système de points, les problèmes et les pressions.*

These are just some of the topics covered by the oral. Let me give you a bit of well-seasoned advice. The oral is about you and not about anybody else in the class. The examiner is not trying to show off their own French. They are trained professionals used to dealing with young people with a finite knowledge of French. Just be yourself. Do your best to answer the questions, and avoid yes or no answers.

Examiner's notes on the Oral section:

For many candidates the vocabulary was the strongest aspect of their performance. Most had mastered a sufficient range of vocabulary to communicate at a basic level on topics concerning their daily lives and the world of young people. At the top end of the scale candidates were not only totally at ease with basic vocabulary themes but had also prepared and had acquired ownership of the terms necessary to deal with more difficult social topics and abstract reasoning. They were willing and able to express their opinions. They also displayed mastery of various idiomatic and elegant expressions, using them appropriately. The *document* frequently provided such candidates with the opportunity to demonstrate the acquisition of the specific vocabulary required for their chosen topic. It is noteworthy that such candidates also had at their disposal a wide range of adjectives. However, some candidates obviously lacked the basic foundation vocabulary required in order to speak about themselves. These vocabulary themes are normally acquired during Junior Cycle, e.g. family, sport, hobbies, where they live, house, school. These candidates had difficulty with everyday vocabulary such as numbers, time, weather, food and school subjects.

Examiners frequently reported an inability to understand basic interrogative words (*qui, quand, pourquoi, comment,* etc.) as a serious barrier to communication. Some candidates failed to recognise key words within a given question, e.g. *Pâques, cet été, l'année dernière*. They had not learnt the very useful *je ne comprends pas* or *voulez-vous répéter la question, s'il vous plaît ?,* which would have avoided at least some of the awkward silences. Examiners frequently mentioned also a poor range of adjectives with excessive reliance on *sympa, super* and *intéressant*.

The most common errors in vocabulary were similar to those noted in previous years. They included:
- Les faux amis: *collège* used instead of *université, facilités* used instead of *installations / équipements*
- Confusion between certain words, e.g. *journée / voyage, travailler / voyager, boisson / besoin, Pâques / bac, chambre / pièce*
- School subjects and names of countries not known
- Inability to mention a favourite dish other than *frites* or *pizza*, or items of clothing bought or received as a present
- Limited range of adjectives and verbs
- Failure to recognise words within the question which hint at the correct tense to be used in answering, e.g. *dernier / prochain, hier / demain*
- Irish words used instead of French words, e.g. *le* for *avec, mar* for *car, nó* for *ou, a lán* for *beaucoup*
- Occasional inappropriate use of slang terms, e.g. *vachement*
- Widespread inability to cope from a lexical point of view once pushed, albeit gently, beyond their comfort zone.

(iii) Structure

Grammar is very important. You need to have a proper grasp of the following tenses:
1. *Présent*
2. *Passé composé*

3. *Imparfait*
4. *Futur*
5. *Conditionnel*
6. *Subjunctive* and the use of pronouns will display advanced learning.

The following was noted in the Chief Examiner's Report, 2010:

As a general rule, this was **not** the most impressive feature of the average candidate's performance in the test. Towards the higher end of the ability range, there were, of course, candidates who demonstrated a wonderful grasp of French grammar. Their basic tenses were correct and they were able to manipulate successfully other verb forms, including compound tenses, the infinitive, the imperfect, the conditional and even at times the present subjunctive. These candidates also displayed accuracy in their use of simple pronouns and the negative form. Unfortunately, other candidates struggled in their efforts to compose short, simple sentences. Candidates are expected to be able manipulate accurately the present, future and past tenses. They should be able to introduce simple pronouns, adjectives and prepositions appropriately and correctly. As in previous years, examiners noted problems in the area of verbs. Some candidates answered all questions in an approximate version of the present tense. Others used *je* at the beginning of all their verbs and followed this by an infinitive. At times, pronunciation of the verb was so distorted that it was impossible for the examiner to be sure of which tense was being attempted. Correct manipulation of the negative form, especially in the *Passé Composé*, was rare.

The most common areas of difficulty were:
- Confusion between the subject pronouns *il* and *elle*
- Total absence of verb, e.g. *Ma famille grande*
- *C'est* and *il y a* confused
- Avoidance of the future tense by over reliance on *je voudrais* or *j'espère* + *infinitive*
- Incorrect word order, e.g. *Ils s'appellent mes sœurs Aoife et Mary*
- Incorrect or unnecessary use of prepositions, e.g. *en Paris, à France, je regarde à la télé, sur samedi, rencontrer avec*
- *Être* used when speaking of age, e.g. *je suis 17 ans*
- Little distinction between definite and indefinite articles
- Expressions of quantity such as *beaucoup* followed by *des* instead of *de*
- Incorrect idiom when speaking of sport and pastimes, e.g. *je joue au sport, je fais natation*
- Confusion regarding expressions of time, e.g. *pendant / pour / depuis*
- Incorrect conjugation of *acheter* and *étudier* in all three basic tenses
- Gender of very common nouns confused or not known, e.g. *la café, le mer*
- Incorrect auxiliary verb or omission of same in *Passé Composé*, e.g. *j'ai allé, je sorti, je ne pas vu*
- Confusion relating to verbs followed by preposition + the infinitive, e.g. *j'espère d'aller*
- Use of *parce que* or *car* confused with *à cause de*, e.g. *parce que mes études* instead of *à cause de mes études*
- Echoing the question form used by the examiner, e.g. *j'allez, je regardez*, etc.

(iv) Communication

Try and keep the conversation going. Remember the more that you can say on a given topic, the less chance the examiner will have to ask you questions. However, it is important to point out that learnt-off reams of information are like a red rag to a bull. The examiner will pick up on this and shoot you down. Stop learning vast amounts on a given topic. Just have a couple of sentences learnt off, so that you have some control over the exam.

The Chief Examiner's Report of 2010 noted the following:

In order to obtain a high mark in this area of the test the candidates must prove by their performance that they are capable of sustaining a natural, flowing and comprehensible conversation in French over twelve minutes. The conversation will deal with the basic details of the candidate's day-to-day life, but will also require the expression of feelings, impressions and opinions. The candidate should have no difficulty in understanding virtually all questions and should give a spontaneous and authentic reply. The candidate should rarely reject any topic proffered by the examiner and there should be no recourse to long extracts learnt by heart. The candidate should be willing and able to take up the challenge of moving beyond the realm of their prepared topics into other related areas. The presentation of the candidate should be such that it would be readily understood by a native speaker of French who has no English. Good pronunciation is, as stated earlier, a prerequisite for efficient communication. Failure to reach an acceptable level of communication was attributed largely to the following factors:

- Unwillingness or hesitancy on the part of some candidates to venture beyond the comfort zone of their prepared script, despite gentle but persistent encouragement from the examiner.
- Over reliance on long sections of learnt-off material or speeches, often introduced *mal à propos* by the candidate. Some candidates seemed frustrated by any attempt from the examiner to judiciously steer the conversation towards a more natural and authentic exchange.
- Tendency to misinterpret the question, often caused by focusing on just one word. The candidate then proceeded to say all that he / she knew on the topic, regardless of its appropriateness as an answer.
- The need to have many questions reformulated.
- Poor overall preparation and perceived lack of interest in French.
- Restricted or erroneous vocabulary, coupled with such inaccurate pronunciation that a native French speaker, with no knowledge of English, would be at a loss to understand what was being said.
- Lack of necessary strategies to overcome any gaps in vocabulary, or lack of opinion on a given subject.

(v) Document option

Candidates may choose to bring in a *document* – a photo, illustration or literary text – for the oral examination. It is not assessed separately, but the candidate's competency in discussing it is taken into account in the final mark. As was the case in previous years, only about half of all candidates availed themselves of this option. In some schools almost every candidate had a *document*, whereas in others no *document* at all was presented.

Most candidates chose to bring in a photograph or illustration. There were not many projects or literary texts. Some candidates seemed unaware that a solid object did not constitute a *document*, and that a photograph should have been used instead. This year, and indeed in recent years, examiners have reported at length on this aspect of the oral test. The following is a summary of their perceptions and conclusions.

A well-prepared *document* was generally advantageous to candidates at all levels of ability. Those who were most competent in the language were afforded an opportunity to shine as they could display their acquisition of more complex vocabulary and structures. The presentation of a well-researched *document* generally greatly enhanced the confidence of less-able students. The security of knowing that their prepared topic would be examined put them more at ease and their performance very often improved subsequently. Some candidates failed to foresee the full range of questions which their chosen topic might provoke. Examiners felt that there were often missed opportunities. A student who chose the topic of a concert, for instance, did not always realise that there would be the possibility to speak about the 'total experience', e.g. getting tickets, transport, friends who also went, venue, accommodation, eating, general atmosphere, weather, bands who played, crowd, return journey, cost, etc.

- Many other candidates patently continued to believe that they would be allowed to recite without interruption their learnt-off material.
- The most frequently chosen topics were foreign holidays, school trips, sport, family events and concerts. Candidates perceived that such topics represented a safe choice. The candidate was secure in the knowledge that their *document* – the subject of which would probably have cropped up in the general conversation anyway – would be given a more extensive airing.
- There were numerous examples of interesting and innovative *documents*. Examples included recent floods, media coverage of Tiger Woods, a poem about racism, the Niall Mellon township trust, a photo of Marie Curie linked to the role of women in society, the Jade Goody story, Poland since World War 2, the effects of the winter of 2010's cold spell, the film *Les Choristes*. The enormous advantage of this type of *document* was that it breathed new life into the conversation and allowed the candidate to display the linguistic talent to cope with a totally different aspect of life.
- The presentation by several members of a class of the same *document* (e.g. trip to Paris) had a tendency to be counter-productive, especially where all candidates had manifestly learnt by heart the same material. Photos of pets or of individuals did not always offer great scope for discussion and development.
- Many candidates who introduced their *document* with a relatively confident opening sentence were incapable of advancing any further. The discussion was then frequently reduced to a description of those in the photo: *Ça, c'est mon ami Paul, il porte un pantalon noir. Il est à droite.* Such candidates had obviously done little preparation, had perhaps chosen the photograph at the last minute, and were definitely not aware of the spirit and intention of the *document* option.
- Almost any subject / topic of the syllabus, including those of everyday relevance to students such as school, family, pastimes, money, can lead to discussion, and thus enable candidates to display a wide-ranging vocabulary and to express feelings and opinions.

Top Ten Tips for the Oral:

1. Remember that this is a conversation and not an interview. The examiner is trained to a very high level, and is there to help you reach your highest potential.
2. Marks are awarded for Structure, Communication, Vocabulary and Pronunciation.
3. Structure applies to how you use your tenses. Using pronouns and the subjunctive is very important to gain maximum points.
4. Communication is how you present yourself. Smile at the examiner, keep eye contact and show a willingness to answer.
5. Vocabulary is really how you phrase your responses. It is not good advice to use slang terms too much. Rich vocabulary is all about using a different way to say something.
6. Pronunciation is very important and accounts for 20% of the exam. I would advise that you listen to French radio and record yourself to perfect your accent.
7. Try to stand out from the rest of the candidates. The material that you will find in *Bonne Chance!* is very different from what you will find elsewhere.
8. Remember that though the oral is a daunting prospect, it is a lot easier than people would have you believe. The examiner knows that French is not spoken in most classrooms. They realise that students find it difficult to speak French naturally, so do not worry!
9. A document is a very good idea if it is well done and you know your subject-matter comprehensively. If you only have a limited understanding of the topic, you will be caught out.
10. All the information for the Oral component can be used in the written section also.

Aural Examination
Listening Comprehension (100 marks)

The CD is common to both Higher and Ordinary Level candidates. The aural test has five sections, with all twenty questions in English, the majority being multi-choice. Section I was the best answered, and less-able candidates scored well here. Section III caused most difficulty. In general, the multiple-choice questions were better attempted than those requiring a written answer.

1. Ask your teacher to test you on previous aurals from years back as far as the early 90s if possible. Listen to your own CDs.
2. Log on to google.fr and type in YouTube in French. Look at any clips in French and even if you don't understand every word, your ear will become accustomed to the language.
3. Log onto www.tf1.fr and listen to 'Le Journal de 13h' or 'Le Journal de 20h' which is a popular news channel on French TV. It would be a fantastic help if your school had interactive whiteboards, and your teacher could play the news for 5 minutes of class a few times a week. If you listen to the news, you will find that a lot of the information is similar to what is happening in Ireland at the moment.
4. Do not leave any blanks in your answer booklet. A guess might be right!
5. Practise saying the key vocabulary given before each listening piece in *Bonne Chance!*
6. Read the question and make sure you understand exactly what you are being asked.

Below is a grid containing 22 years of material from the aural exam. Note that the 5 sections were introduced in 1997. Prior to that year, there were only 4 sections in the Aural. If you read through the various topics, you will see that sport is quite popular, as are holidays and relationships between teenagers and parents.

AURAL EXAMINATION 1992 – 2013

Year	Section I	Section II	Section III	Section IV	Section V
2013	3 French teenagers talk about a journey around Europe with their parents.	An interview with Guy, a young French farmer, about his life.	A conversation between two teenagers, Valérie and Hervé about pet.	An interview with Marie-Amélie Le Fur, who won a gold medal at the 2012 Paralympics.	Minister Hélène Conway-Mouret. Demonstrators in Nantes. A fire in Montpellier.
2012	French student on language stay in Galway.	Relationship with teenage children.	School subjects and career choices.	Speeding and motor offences.	Weather. Drugs. Parachutist.
2011	Country V's. Urban living.	Work and looking for a job.	Borrowing a car. Teenage problems.	First woman astronaut. Interview.	Attack. Car ferries. Missing child.
2010	Work in Australia. Family. Going out at night.	Interview with an archaeologist.	Louise is moving into a new house. What issues will she face?	Tourism in Paris and people's livelihoods.	Road accident. New internet laws. Supermarket recalls toy.
2009	Mobile phones.	Interview with Alain, Olympic swimmer.	Losing a bag in a café.	Winning the lottery. Valérie Guénot.	Tornado victims & Carrefour Hijackers. Penalties for failing to use indicators.
2008	Interview with Sophie Marceau about independence.	Interview with long-distance lorry driver.	2 friends visit Ireland and argue then separate.	3 rugby pros who left their countries to join clubs in France.	Record sales. Wild boar on rampage. Police action.
2007	High cost of holidays.	Interview with Bernard Kouchner about civic national service scheme.	Boyfriend/ girlfriend discussing an issue.	Consequences of a fire in Rouen.	Lottery win. Cocaine seizure. Weather forecast.
2006	Interview with Jamel about school and success in life.	Interview with an expert on languages.	Family matters. Buying a present for a father.	Interview with Nathalie, about women in politics.	Sport. Teenager injured. People arrested.

2005	Interview with Julien, contestant in 'Nouvelle Star'.	Interview with Thierry Henry.	Memorable moment in the life of a father.	Moving out of home to go to Uni. Brother and sister talk.	Train evacuation. Consumer product French banning of product.
2004	Girl accused of stealing something.	Interview with estate agent about buying in France.	Special Olympics in Ireland.	UN rights of the child interview.	Grape harvest. Broadband. Incident involving a child.
2003	Interview with a weather forecaster.	School staying open during the summer.	Interview with a pro cyclist.	Talk between mother and son about new apartment in Paris.	Vehicle strike. George Michael writing song.
2002	Interview with mother about son's language stay in England.	Tour operators and cost of holidays.	Interview with French Sociologist on the 35 hour working week.	New school for a girl from Paris to a small town in Burgundy.	Strike. Fault with new coins. Result of research.
2001	Move from Paris – Provence Jean Galais.	Giving up smoking.	2 girls discuss their boyfriends.	Teenage violence.	Traffic problem. Ministerial measure. Sentence imposed.
2000	French orienteering interview.	Interview with Axelle Red.	Problems at home and at school for teenagers.	Low cost holiday scheme.	Protest Public transport Internet. Waste disposal. Drugs Consumer rights.
1999	Interview with song writer.	Interview about the history of the Arc de Triomphe.	Olympic medalist talks about the countdown to a big competition.	Interview with sociologist about 'l'identité Bretonne'.	Strike. Car industry. Wine producers.
1998	Interview with a paralympic champion.	Interview with Isabelle Adjani and Cannes festival.	Interview about motherhood & women's education.	Interview about foreigners who holiday in France.	Farmer's fruit. North pole trip.
1997	Interview with person who set up dog minding service.	Interview with Olympic games athlete.	Interview with French fire fighter.	Interview with a member of French government.	Protest. Accidents and weather. Refugees.
1996	Laure Panore, gifted school girl & career.	Interview with McDonalds manager.	Interview with sociologist about young people.	Interview with French goalkeeper.	

1995	France during the war.	Interview with a writer.	Interview with General about Bosnian war.	Sports injuries.
1994	Radio show 'à votre service'.	Interview about scrambling bikes.	Interview with Yves Duteil, singer.	New types of holidays in France.
1993	Marc Vassal and the Bateaux Mouches in Paris.	Interview with 'Dark', a grafitti artist talks about his work.	Interview about position of women in professional life.	Princess Caroline of Monaco moves to a French town.
1992	Job interview.	Gilles Vigneault talks about Quebec.	Pets and astronauts 2 news items.	McDonalds/plastic containers and the environment.

Ordinary Level Leaving Cert Exam Paper

Layout of exam:
- Written – 220 marks
- Oral – 80 marks
- Aural – 100 marks

The French Ordinary Level examination comprises three components – Written, Aural and Oral. The Written paper consists of two sections – Reading Comprehension and Written Expression.

Written Examination
Section I – Compréhension Écrite (160 marks)
There are four questions, each worth 40 marks. All four questions must be answered. The first section is the **Compréhension Écrite** and is worth 160 marks, or 40% of the entire exam.

In this section, you must answer four comprehension texts, and complete each one. Remember that a question asked in English must be answered in English, unless you are asked for the title of a book or film. Keep a vocabulary notebook, and break this vocabulary into topics, as is done in *Bonne Chance!* The first two comprehensions will be in English and the final two will be in French. It is important that when you attempt the reading comprehensions, you read the heading, the questions and the sub-heading if there is one. Once you have done this, take a highlighter, box off each section, and then attempt the questions related to the particular section. Psychologically, this gives you more control over the text. The topics in the comprehension section vary greatly from year to year. They may be from newspapers, magazines, book or film reviews, entertainment news, interviews etc.

Section II – Production Écrite (60 marks)

This section is worth 60 marks or 15%. You are given three different sections, each with a choice of two different options, (a) or (b). You must choose two of the three sections and complete one question from each of the two that you have chosen.

A. is usually a fill in the blanks or a form filling exercise. (30 marks)
B. is usually a postcard or a message. (30 marks, 15 language, 15 communication)
C. is usually a diary entry (30 marks, communication 15 marks, language 15 marks) or a formal letter. (layout 6 marks, language 12 marks, communication 12 marks)

Section A
(a) – Cloze Test (30 marks)
This question is usually attempted by most students.

(b) – Form Filling
Generally speaking, questions 1–5 of this choice are well answered. Many of the longer questions are based on work which candidates would have prepared for the Oral, so they would have had the added benefit of approaching this section with confidence. Misspelling is a common error with inattention to verbs, tenses and vocabulary.

Section B
(a) – Message
This was a less popular choice than Section B (b). The tenses and vocabulary required were problematic for many candidates.

(b) – Postcard
This was a more popular choice than Section B (a).
Poor verbs, spellings and vocabulary were evident.
Many candidates include paragraphs of extraneous material for which no marks can be given.

Section C
(a) – Diary
Language marks awarded were low. A lack of knowledge of tenses, agreements, vocabulary and spelling accounted for this.

(b) – Formal Letter
This was the least popular choice of all the written questions. Specific marks for Layout were awarded here as well as marks for Communication and Language.
Top of page: Many merited 1 mark for general layout. Errors included omission of the year and / or *Irlande*. The incorrect salutation *Cher monsieur / madame* was often used.

Closing formula: Be careful to learn a strong closing statement, as marks are generally lost here. Again, marks are usually lost for simple mistakes in tenses and verb agreement. If students choose to attempt this question, they would need to learn the layout of a formal letter, and thus gain a potential 6 marks.

Ordinary Level Aural (100 marks)

The Ordinary Level listening exam is worth 100 marks and has 5 sections. The Listening Comprehension takes place about 15 minutes after completion of the Written Exam. The Listening Comprehension lasts approximately 40 minutes. The CD is common for both Ordinary and Higher with different questions for each level. In most of the questions, the student is faced with a multiple choice, where the candidate is required to tick the correct box. The students will either hear the individual listening pieces two or three times. All the questions for the Aural Section are asked in English and must be answered in English. The recordings vary between interviews, news reports, conversations or opinions.

Ordinary Level Oral (80 marks)

The Ordinary Level oral exam is tested in exactly the same way as the Honours Level, except that your results are converted after the Written Exam in June. The exam itself takes between 12 and 15 minutes. The oral examiner does not know which candidates are doing Ordinary Level and which are doing Higher Level. Please read the breakdown of the Oral Examination under the Higher Level section.

Useful Websites

Here is a list of useful websites to expand your learning and enjoyment of French.

www.schooloffrench.ie
This is the author's own website which includes sample opinion pieces, letters and diary entries. There is also an extensive grammar section, which students may download for free.

www.wordreference.com
This website is excellent when you are stuck on a particular word or phrase. There is also a very useful forum, where nuances of the french language are explored.

www.examinations.ie
This website includes all that a student needs pertaining to the Irish State Examinations.

www.french.ie
This website is a portal site created by and for French teachers in Ireland and is part of the broader Scoilnet portal. The site aims to provide resource material for teachers and the opportunity to consult pedagogical material online.

www.tf1.fr
This is a french news website, which students can access and watch current affairs and news reports. Very useful for exposing students to vocabulary used in Leaving Cert Aural Section V.

www.lefigaro.fr
This website links students to the french broadsheet *Le Figaro*, and contains interesting cultural and topical articles.

www.lemonde.fr
This website links students to the french broadsheet *Le Monde* and like *Le Figaro*, contains very interesting cultural and topical articles.

www.1jour1actu.com
This website is especially designed for students, as it takes a topical issue and explains it in a clear and concise fashion.

www.alliance-francaise.ie
The aim of the Alliance Française in Dublin is to promote French culture, as well as to provide a space for intercultural exchanges between Ireland and the cultures of the French-speaking world.

www.parismatch.com
This website is a French weekly magazine. It covers major national and international news along with celebrity lifestyle features.

www.lequipe.fr
This website is dedicated to all things sport.

www.liberation.fr
This newspaper is originally left-wing, and was founded by the French philosopher and existentialist Jean-Paul Sartre.

If you are using the eBook, look out for this icon at the end of each chapter. These link directly to extra online worksheets for this chapter on gillmacmillan.ie.

CHAPITRE 1 — La famille

Aural Section

A Je vous présente ma famille

Français	Anglais	How to pronounce
un attaché commercial	a sales representative	an ah-tah-shay comm-mer-see-al
des surgelés	frozen food	day sur jel lay
râler (regular er verb)	to grumble or to complain	ral-lay
grommeler (regular er verb)	to grumble or to mutter	grom-meh-lay
soûler (regular er verb)	to make one's head spin	sue-lay
être désordonné	to be messy	et-re day zor don ay
toucher	to affect or to earn or to receive	too-shay
travailler d'arrache-pied	to work very hard	tra-vy-ay dar-rash pea-ay
joindre les deux bouts	to make ends meet	jowan-dre lay duh boo
kinésithérapeute	physiotherapist	kin-niz-zee-tear-rah-poot

Three people talk about their families. Listen and fill in the grid.

Question	Charlotte	Jean-Claude	Jennifer
1. Who is studying a lot at the moment?			✓
2. Which person gets on very well with their mother?		✓	
3. Whose father works in a rehabilitation centre?			✓
4. Who finds it hard to go out?		✓	
5. Who needs to get almost 600 points?			✓
6. Who has to do a lot of work at home?	✓		
7. Which person has brothers who are untidy?	✓		
8. Who is the eldest?	✓		
9. Who wants to become a solicitor?	✓	✓	
10. Whose father is a sales representative?		✓	✓
11. Who is an only child?	✓	✓	
12. Who has everything that they need?		✓	

B Les disputes en famille

Français	Anglais	How to pronounce
taquiner	to tease	tack-key-nay
être claqué	to be really tired	et-re clack-ay
ça y est	that's it	sigh-yeh

Four people ring an agony aunt to talk about disputes that they are having concerning family life. Please listen and fill in the grid.

Nom	Le problème	Avec qui doit-il/elle parler	Quel conseil a été donné ?
1. Christophe Duchamp	Can't study	Because of his two little brothers.	Speak to your parents.
2. Florence	Girls in her class are teasing her.	Because her dad is unemployed.	Speak to the principal
3. Madame Jeannot	2 To kids argueing	Talk to husband	Tell them that is it
4. Marc Voinot			

C Les parents stricts

Français	Anglais	How to pronounce
avoir hâte	to desire or to wish	av-war at
en ce qui concerne	concerning	on-se-key concern
flemmarder	to hang about	fle-mar-day
mettre l'accent sur	to emphasise	mett lak-son sewer
quelqu'un	someone	kel-can

Est-ce que vous vous entendez bien avec vos parents ?

Qui dit Quoi ?

Statement	Louise	David	Suzanne
My life is a chore now	✓		
I am lucky that I get on well with them			
I have quite a lot of freedom		✓	
I can't wait to finish this hellish year	✓		
My father and I share the same interests			✓
I have to go straight home	✓	✓	
We all eat together		✓	
I no longer have the right to laze about in town with my friends	✓		
It depends			✓
They have always been like that	✓	✓	
They talk to me a lot			✓
Concerning study	✓		

Bonne Chance !

D Les familles monoparentales

Français	Anglais	How to pronounce
au sein de	*within*	oh san duh
la précarité	*precarity*	la pre-ca-ree-tay
la dure réalité	*the harsh reality*	la dur ray-al-lee-tay
la moitié	*half*	la mwat-tee-ay

Answer the questions below.

1. What percentage of families are headed up by the mother?
2. Why is the number of single-parent families growing?
3. What risks do single-parent families present?
4. What percentage of mothers in single-parent families work full-time?
5. In what way are their living conditions different from those of two-parent families?
6. What percentage of these families share their accommodation with others?

E L'échange des bébés à la naissance

Français	Anglais	How to pronounce
rien	*nothing*	ree-an
liés	*linked*	lee-ay
quitter	*to leave*	key-tay
présent	*present*	prez-zon
gérer	*to manage*	jeh-ray
biologique	*biological*	bee-olo-jeek
au cours de	*during*	oh-coor-de
encore	*still, yet, again*	on-core

Écoutez le rapport et puis répondez aux questions.

1. Qu'est-ce qui s'est passé il y a quatorze ans ?
2. Quels genres de tests ont été réalisé ?
3. Qu'est-ce que les deux filles ont décidé de faire ?
4. Combien d'argent réclament les familles ?
5. Qu'est-ce que la juge a dit ?
6. Qu'est-ce qu'une des deux mères a dit en rencontrant sa fille biologique ?
7. Quelle est la religion mentionnée dans le texte ?

Chapitre 1 La famille

F Les allocations familiales

Français	Anglais	How to pronounce
Les allocations familiales	*child benefit*	lays al-low-cass-yon fam-milly-al
aisé(e)	*well-off*	ay-zay
mensuel	*monthly*	mon-sue-el
inaperçu(e)	*unnoticed*	in-ah-per-sue
supprimer	*to delete or remove*	sue-preem-may

Le gouvernement français baissera les allocations familiales. Remplissez les blancs.

Je ne _____ pas que diviser par deux les allocations _____ des ménages dits « aisés » soit une _____ chose. Je trouve même cela très injuste. Je ne ____ pas que ma situation soit assez confortable. À _____ deux, mon mari et moi _____ à peu près 7,000 euros nets par mois. Nous avons deux enfants et nous _____127 euros mensuels de la _____ de la CAF. Et croyez-moi, ce _____ pas de l'argent qui passe inaperçu. Nous vivons en _____ parisienne, où il faut _____ calculer. Une fois qu'on a payé les _____ l'électricité, le crédit pour notre _____, la nourriture et les frais _____, il ne nous reste pas non plus _____-chose. À l'école, tous les _____ tels que la cantine ou les activités _____ sont calculés sur notre _____ familial, du coup, nous payons plein ____ . Par exemple, pour les _____ de tennis de _____ nous avons le tarif le plus élevé : ____ euros par an. Ce sont les allocations familiales qui nous _____ à en payer une partie. Sans les allocations familiales, je ne dis pas que nous _____, loin de là, mais il nous faudrait _____ quelque part. Je ne pense pas qu'il _____ judicieux de toucher aux allocations familiales pour les _____ comme moi. J'ai le sentiment _____ à une classe déjà _____ ponctionnée comme ça. Les _____ non plus ne sont pas responsables de la _____, et supprimer des _____ accordées à leurs parents pour les _____, c'est, au final, les pénaliser eux.

G Le conflit entre générations

Français	Anglais	How to pronounce
tout à fait	*completely*	toot-ah-fay
des crises	*crises*	day kreeze
lorsque	*when, as soon as, while*	lorsk
aussi	*also*	oh-see
indéboulonnable	*unmovable*	an-de-boo-lon-abl
une aile	*a wing*	oone el
éviter	*to avoid*	ay-vee-tay

Answer the questions below.

Section 1.
1. What is completely normal and inevitable?
2. What do parents pretend to forget?

Section 2.
1. How long have people been talking about a conflict of generations?
2. When children are in conflict with their parents, name one feeling that they experience.

Section 3.
1. Name one thing that teenagers rebel against.
2. Name one thing that parents refuse to see.
3. Why do parents refuse to give up?

H Leaving Cert 2012 Section II

Français	Anglais	How to pronounce
le conflit	*conflict*	le con-flee
s'inquiéter	*to worry*	sang-kee-et-ay
la guerre	*the war*	la gair
être convaincu	*to be convinced*	et-re con-van-coo
ensemble	*together*	on-sombl

You will now hear three parents, Serge, Hélène and Victor, each talking about their relationship with their teenage child. The material will be played three times: first right through, then in three segments with pauses, and finally right through again.

1. What does Serge's son do when his father tries to speak to him?
2. According to Hélène, her daughter
    (a) was not working enough at school
    (b) was watching too much television

Chapitre 1 La famille

(c) was unwilling to help at home
(d) was going out too often with her friends.

3. (i) What country did Victor and his son visit?
   (ii) Victor is convinced that parents should
   (a) give money to their children
   (b) discipline their children
   (c) play games with their children
   (d) spend time with their children.

I Les faits divers

Français	Anglais	How to pronounce
tout seul	*all alone*	too-sul
le soulagement	*relief*	le sue-lage-mon
un otage	*a hostage*	an oh-taje
la foudre	*lightning*	la foud-re
un incendie	*a fire*	an ann-sahn dee
sain et sauf	*safe and sound*	san ay sof

First Piece
1. When was the child discovered?
2. Why did the parents of the child not realise that he had disappeared?

Second Piece
1. When were the hostages released?
2. When had they been kidnapped?

Third Piece
1. Where was the teenager when he was hit by lightning?

Fourth Piece
1. Why were these children thrown from a window?
2. What happened to them?

Bonne Chance!

Oral Section – *Let's Get Talking*
Ten common questions asked on the subject of the family

Français	Anglais	How to pronounce
Parlez-moi un peu de votre famille	*Speak to me a little about your family*	par-lay moi an puh de vot-re fam-mee.
Vous-êtes combien dans votre famille ?	*How many are in your family?*	vooz-et com-bee-en don vot-re fam-mee?
Avez-vous des frères et des sœurs ?	*Do you have any brothers and sisters?*	ah-vey voo day frair ay day seur?
Est-ce que vous vous entendez bien avec vos parents / votre frère / votre sœur ?	*Do you get on well with your parents / your brother / your sister?*	esse-kuh voo vooz on-ton-day be-en avek voh par-ron / vot-re frair / vot-re soeur?
Quels avantages / inconvénients y a-t-il à être enfant unique ?	*What advantages / disadvantages are there in being an only child?*	kel ah-von-taj / an-con-ven-yon ee-ah-teel ah et-re on-fon oo-neek?
Est-ce que le fait que vous soyez l'aîné(e) de la famille vous responsibilise ?	*Does the fact that you are the eldest of the family make you responsible?*	esse-kuh le fay kuh vooz swa-yay lainay de la fam-mee voo ress-pon-se-bil-eez?
À propos de quoi vous disputez-vous ?	*What do you argue about?*	ah pro-po de kwah voo dis-poot-ay voo?
Qu'est-ce que vous aimez faire en famille ?	*What do you like to do as a family?*	kess-kuh vooz em-may fair on fam-mee?
Vous êtes le cadet / la cadette de la famille. Est-ce que cela est un avantage ou un inconvénient ?	*You are the youngest in the family. Is this an advantage or a disadvantage?*	vooz-et le cad-day / la ca-dett de la fam-mee. Esse-kuh sel-la et an ah-von-taj oo an an-con-ven-yon?
Parlez-moi un peu de votre mère / votre père	*Talk to me a little about your mother / your father.*	par-lay moi an puh de vote mair / vote pair.

Dix questions et réponses possibles sur la famille

1. **Parlez-moi un peu de votre famille.**

Je viens d'une famille typiquement irlandaise	I come from a typical Irish family
Je suis membre d'une famille nombreuse	I am from a big family
Je vis dans une famille mono-parentale	I live in a single-parent family
Je suis issu(e) d'une petite famille	I am from a small family
Je suis l'aîné(e) de la famille	I am the eldest in the family
Je suis au mileu	I am in the middle
Je suis le/la benjamin(e) de la famille	I am the youngest in the family
Je suis enfant unique	I am an only child

2. **Vous-êtes combien dans votre famille ?**

Ma famille comprend 6 personnes	My family is made up of 6 people
Il y a 5 personnes dans ma famille	There are 5 people in my family
Nous sommes 4 dans ma famille	We are 4 people in my family

3. **Avez-vous des frères et des sœurs ?**

Oui, j'ai un frère et une sœur	Yes, I have one brother and one sister
Je n'ai pas de frères ni de sœurs	I do not have any brothers or sisters
J'ai un frère seulement	I have only one brother

4. **Est-ce que vous vous entendez bien avec vos parents/votre frère/votre sœur ?**

Je m'entends très bien / assez bien /mal avec mes parents / mon frère /ma sœur / mes frères et sœurs	I get on very well / quite well / badly with my parents / my brother / my sister / my brothers and sisters.
Je me dispute souvent avec…	I argue a lot with…
Je partage des moments de bonheur avec…	I have a great time with…
Je me dispute de temps en temps avec…	I sometimes argue with…
Mes parents sont facile à vivre	My parents are easy-going
Mes parents sont très exigents	My parents are very demanding
Mes parents me font confiance	My parents trust me
Mes parents n'arrêtent pas de me gronder	My parents never stop telling me off
Mes parents travaillent tous les deux, donc j'ai pas mal de liberté	Both my parents work so I have quite a bit of freedom
Mon père est au chômage donc la vie n'est pas très facile en ce moment	My father is unemployed so life isn't very easy at the moment

Ma mère vient de perdre son boulot donc la famille est sous pression financièment	My mother has just lost her job so the family is under pressure financially
Mes parents sont divorcés donc je partage ma vie entre deux maisons	My parents are divorced so I share my life between two houses
Ma sœur/mon frère m'embête continuellement	My sister/my brother is always annoying me
Mon frère/ma sœur me donne un coup de main avec les devoirs car il/elle a fini l'école et il/elle va à l'université	My brother/sister gives me a hand with my homework because he/she has finished school and he/she is going to university

5. **Quels avantages/inconvénients y a-t-il à être enfant unique ?**
Je suis enfant unique. Il y a bien sûr des pours et des contres. J'aurais aimé avoir des frères ou des sœurs avec qui j'aurais pu partager des moments de bonheur, mais c'est la vie. J'ai tout ce qu'il me faut et je m'entends très bien avec me parents.
I am an only child. Of course there are advantages and disadvantages. I would have liked to have had brothers or sisters with whom I could have shared moments of happiness, but that's life. I have everything that I need and I get on really well with my parents.

6. **Est-ce que le fait que vous soyez l'aîné(e) de la famille vous responsibilise ?**
Je suis l'aîné(e) de la famille. D'être l'aîné a des pours et des contres. Mes parents me font confiance mais en même temps ils exigent que je donne le bon exemple. Mes frères me soûlent parfois. Ils sont désordonnés et ils me tapent sur les nerfs ! La vie en famille n'est pas toujours facile. Ma mère me gronde et mon père se met à grommeler si je ne fais pas ce qu'ils me demandent de faire. Mais dans l'ensemble, je m'entends très bien avec eux.
I am the eldest in the family. Being the eldest has its advantages and disadvantages. My parents trust me but at the same time, they expect me to give a good example. My brothers annoy me sometimes. They are messy and they get on my nerves. Family life is not always easy. My mother gives out to me and my father grumbles away if I don't do what they ask me. But, overall I get on very well with them.

7. **À propos de quoi vous disputez-vous ?**
Comme n'importe quelle famille, nous nous disputons de temps en temps. Je me mets en colère si ma sœur pique mes vêtements, ou si mon frère laisse traîner ses affaires. Ma mère veut que la maison soit bien rangée et elle me gronde si les choses ne sont pas à leur place. Le soir, c'est difficile de regarder son émission favorite, car tout le monde veut voir une émission différente.
Like any family we argue from time to time. I get angry if my sister robs my clothes or if my brother leaves his stuff lying around. My mother wants the house to be tidy and she tells me off if things are not in their place. In the evening, it is difficult to watch one's favourite programme, because everyone wants to watch a different programme.

8. **Qu'est-ce que vous aimez faire en famille ?**
Ma famille est très active et nous aimons faire un tas de chose. Nous sommes membre d'un centre de loisirs et presque tous les weekends, nous faisons des activités comme par exemple le ski nautique ou l'aviron. Nous prenons la voiture tous les weekends, pour rendre visite à mes grand-parents qui habitent à la campagne. J'adore

aller en ville avec ma mère et mon frère aime bien faire du jardinage avec mon père, car ils ont tous les deux la main verte.

My family is very active and we like to do a load of things. We are members of a leisure centre and almost every weekend, we do activities like for example water-skiing or rowing. We take the car every week to visit my grandparents who live in the countryside. I love to go to town with my mother and my brother likes to do some gardening with my father, as they both have green fingers.

9. **Vous êtes le cadet/la cadette de la famille. Est-ce que cela est un avantage ou un inconvénient ?**

    Tout le monde est de l'avis que les benjamins ont une vie bénie des dieux. Je ne suis pas tout à fait convaincu(e) que cela soit vraiment le cas. Mes parents me traitent comme un bébé et mes frères et sœurs ne m'écoutent jamais. Ceci dit, c'est également vrai que je peux sortir quand je veux car mes parents ont déjà parcouru ce chemin avec les autres. C'est une une voie toute tracée d'avance.

    Everybody thinks that the youngest children have a charmed existence. I am not at all convinced that this is entirely right. My parents treat me like a baby and my brothers and sisters never listen to me. Having said this, it is also true that I can go out when I like as my parents have already been down this road with the others. It is a well worn path at this stage.

10. **Parlez-moi un peu de votre mère/votre père.**

    Ma mère est de nature calme et elle est très comprehensive. Je peux lui parler de tout. Elle travaille très dure à la maison et elle fait en sorte que nous soyons tous heureux. C'est une vraie mère poule.

    My mother has a calm disposition and she is very understanding. I can talk to her about everything. She works hard at home and she makes sure that we are all happy. She is a real mother hen.

    Mon père est très drôle. Il travaille en tant que pompier et je sais que ce métier peut être assez dangereux. Il a bon caractère et il est généreux avec l'esprit ouvert. Il comprend les gens et il nous aide à être tolérants dans la vie.

    My father is very funny. He works as a fireman and I know that this job can be quite dangerous. He is good-humoured and he is generous with an open mind. He understands people and he helps us to be tolerant in life.

Le Vocabulaire Essentiel

Français	Anglais	How to pronounce
la mère	the mother	la mair
le père	the father	le pair
le fils	the son	le feece
la fille	the daughter	la fee
la grand-mère	the grandmother	la gron-mair
le grand-père	the grandfather	le gron-pair
le cousin	the cousin (m)	le coo-zan
la cousine	the cousin (f)	la coo-zine
la tante	the aunt	la tont
l'oncle	the uncle	lonk-le
la belle-sœur	the sister-in-law	la bell-sir
le beau-frère	the brother-in-law	le bow-frair
le parrain	the godfather	le par-ran
la marraine	the godmother	la mar-wren
le frère	the brother	le frair
la sœur	the sister	la seur
la petite-fille	the granddaughter	la pet-teet fee
le petit-fils	the grandson	le peh tee feece
l'aîné(e)	the eldest	lain-nay
le cadet/la cadette	the youngest	le ka-day / la ka-dett
le mariage	marriage	le mar-ree-aje
le divorce	divorce	le dee-vorce
une famille nombreuse	a big family	oone fam-mee nom-bruz
une famille mono-parentale	a single-parent family	oone fam-mee mono-par-ron-tal
l'enfance	childhood	lon-fonce
la jeunesse	youth	la jeun-ness
la vie d'adulte	adulthood	la vee dad-dult
le troisième âge	old age	le trwoz-ee-em aje
les fiançailles (f)	engagement	lay fe- onsigh
les noces (f)	wedding	lay noce
les obsèques	funeral	lays ob-seq
utile	useful	ooh-teal
très	very	tray or trez if followed by a vowel
c'est	it is	say

Chapitre 1 La famille

French	English	Pronunciation
la moitié	half	la mwot-tee-ay
mes	my	may or mays if followed by a vowel
mais	but	may
toujours	always / yet / still	two-joor
travailler	to work	tra-vy-ay
la mort	death	la maur
la naissance	birth	la nay-sonce
un jumeau	twin-boy	ann jou-mo
une jumelle	twin-girl	oone jou-mel
des jumeaux	twins (boy + girl or 2 boys)	day jou-mo
des jumelles	twins (girls)	day jou-mel
enfant unique	only child	on-fon ooh-neek
la femme	wife / woman	la fam
le mari	husband	le mah-ree
l'époux	husband	lay pou
l'épouse	wife	lay pooze
prévenir	to warn	pray-ven-near
faire des histoires	to make a fuss	fair days is-twar
une bataille	a battle	oone bat-tye
parler	to speak	par-lay
la communication	communication	la com-mune-nee-cass-yon
abriter	to shelter	ah-bree-tay
loin	far	lwan
proche	near	prush
à côté	beside	ah co-tay
vivre au sein de la famille	to live within the family	veev-re oh sain de la fam-mee
quitter la famille	to leave the family	key-tay la fam-mee
la tête de la famille	the head of the family	la tet de la fam-mee
bouleverser	to upset / to disrupt	bool-ver-say
les intentions	intentions	lays an-tonce-yon
le bonheur conjugal	wedded bliss	le bon-eur con-ju-gal
le soulagement	relief	le sue-laje-mon
revendiquer	to claim / to demand	re-von-dee-kay
la discipline	discipline	la diss-see-plean
la dépendance	dependency	la day-pon-donce
l'adolescence	adolescence	lah-doh-less-sonce
une pomme de discorde	a bone of contention	oone pum de diss-cord
en discorde	in disagreement	on diss-cord
un logement	accommodation	le loge-mon

aisé	*well-off*	aze-ay
le foyer	*the home*	le fwoy-ay
les parents biologiques	*the biological parents*	lay par-ron bee-ol-oh-jeek
la materité	*the maternity*	la ma-ter-nee-tay
une grossesse	*a pregnancy*	oone grow-cess
la vie quotidienne	*daily life*	la vee ko-tid-dee-en
le chiffre	*the figure*	le sheaf-re
le ménage	*household*	le men-aje
la fragilité	*fragility*	la fra-jil-lee-tay
la réalité	*reality*	la ray-al-lee-tay
les régles	*rules*	lay regl
déranger	*to upset / to disturb*	day-ron-jay
regarder la télé	*to watch TV*	re-gar-day la tellay
une corvée	*chore*	oone cor-vay
sortir	*to go out*	sor-teer
strict	*strict*	streect
taquiner	*to tease, to annoy*	tack-key-nay
se bagarrer	*to argue*	se bag-gar-ray
souvent	*often*	sue-von
les disputes	*arguments*	lay diss-peute
femme au foyer	*a housewife*	fam-oh-fwoy-ay
parfois	*sometimes*	par-fwah
un tas	*a pile*	an tah
s'entendre avec	*to get on with*	sawn-tond-re avec
dans l'ensemble	*overall*	don-lon-somb
gronder	*to tell (someone) off*	ral-lay
typiquement	*typically*	tip-peak-mon

Dix constructions clés sur la famille

1. **Je peux vous dire que = *I can tell you that***
   Je peux vous dire que ce n'est pas toujours facile de partager sa chambre avec quelqu'un.
   I can tell you that it is not always easy to share one's room with someone.

2. **Dans l'ensemble = *overall***
   Bien sur dans n'importe quelle famille, il y a des hauts et des bas, mais dans l'ensemble nous nous entendons très bien.
   Of course in any family there are ups and downs, but overall, we get on very well.

3. **C'est à dire = *that is to say***
   Je voudrais parler le français assez couramant, c'est à dire sans faire trop de fautes.
   I would like to speak French quite fluently, that is to say without making too many mistakes.

4. **Arriver à faire quelque chose** = *to manage to do something*
   Je ne sais pas si Jean arrivera à tout faire avant l'arrivée de sa tante.
   I don't know if John will manage to do everything before his aunt's arrival.

5. **Il faut que + subjunctive of the verb faire** = *I must do (it is necessary that I do)*
   Il faut que je fasse de mon mieux si je veux obtenir un maximum de points au bac.
   I must do my best if I want to get maximum points in the leaving certificate.

6. **Afin de** = *in order to*
   Les parents travaillent d'arrache-pied afin de donner tout ce qu'ils peuvent aux enfants.
   The parents work very hard in order to give everything that they can to the children.

7. **De toute façon** = *in any case*
   Dans ma famille tout le monde doit donner un coup de main à la maison avec le ménage. Je trouve que c'est mieux et de toute façon, ma mère n'est pas une esclave.
   In my family, everyone has to give a hand in the house with the work. I find that it is better and, in any case, my mother is not a slave.

8. **Avoir hâte de faire quelque chose** = *to look forward to doing something*
   (Remember when using expressions containing verbs, the verb is generally put into the tense being used.)
   Il a hâte de retourner dans sa famille après avoir travaillé à l'étranger.
   He is looking forward to returning to his family after having worked abroad.

9. **En ce qui concerne** = *regarding or concerning*
   Je ne sais pas ce que le gouvernement va faire en ce qui concerne les allocations familiales.
   I do not know what the government is going to do regarding child benefit.

10. **Avoir de la chance** = *to be lucky*
    J'ai de la chance d'avoir une famille qui me soutient sans hésitation.
    I am lucky to have a family which supports me without hesitation.

Dix expressions authentiques et ludiques

1. Il m'en a fait voir des vertes et des pas mures = *he messed me around with all sorts of excuses*
2. Faire une conduite de Grenoble = *to throw someone out, to receive someone in a hostile manner*
3. Vivre chichement = *to live frugally, with the suggestion of avarice*
4. Une guerre picrocholine = *a conflict between people or institutions for obscure or ridiculous reasons*
5. Faire avancer le schmilblick = *to progress in finding a solution*
6. Envoyer paître = *to get rid of someone rudely*
7. L'arbre qui cache la forêt = *you can't see the wood for the trees*
8. Un rond-de-cuir = *someone who works in an office*
9. Une autre paire de manches = *a completely different story*
10. De gré ou de force = *by hook or by crook*

CHAPITRE 2
Les amis et l'amitié

Aural Section

A. Décrivez votre meilleur ami

Français	Anglais	How to pronounce
meilleur(e)	best	may-er
une infirmière	a nurse	oone an-fir-me-air
la confiance	trust	la con-fee-once
des conseils	advice	day con-say
coquin	mischievous	co-kah
un immeuble	a block of flats	an ee-mubl

Écoutez ces trois jeunes qui décrivent leur meilleur(e) ami(e). Vous allez entendre trois personnes qui parlent de leur meilleur ami. Écoutez et remplissez la grille.

La phrase	François	Émilie	Fatima
For me, friendship is sacred			✓
She understands me like no-one else		✓	
We grew up in an HLM in Beauval			✓
I trust her		✓	
I feel like I have always known Luc	✓		
We see each other every day	✓		
We have experienced a lot of things together	✓		✓
That's life		✓	
I am lucky to have			✓
I have known her since the age of 12.	✓		

depuis

B L'amitié est sacrée

Français	Anglais	How to pronounce
l'amitié	*friendship*	lah-mee-tee-ay
compter	*to count*	con-tay
se confier	*to confide in*	se con-fee-ay
conseiller	*to advise*	con-say-yay
une enquête	*a survey*	oone on-kett
essentiel	*essential*	ay-sahn-see-el
depuis	*for / since*	de-pwee

Answer the questions below.

1. Selon l'auteur qui sont les amis? [*According to*] [*who are*]
2. Quand est-ce qu'il ne faut pas compter? [*When*] [*it is not necessary*]
3. Qui a mené l'enquête? L'---------- N----------de la S-------------et des é-----é-------------- [*Who led*]
4. Grâce aux _____ technologies, les amis _____ rester en _____ en permanence. [*Thanks to*]
5. Qu'est-ce que les jeunes aiment bien? [*what*] [*Youth*]
6. Les enfants qui ont des liens forts apprenent quoi exactement? [*Who have connections*] [*strong*] [*learn what*]

C La pression des pairs

Français	Anglais	How to pronounce
les pairs	*peers*	lay pair
persuader	*to persuade*	per-swed-day
les mœurs	*customs, habits, lifestyles*	lay murse
heureusement	*fortunately*	er-reuz-mon

Écrivez chaque phrase en français avec l'aide du CD:

Statement	Numéro
1. several people try to persuade	
2. you can be subjected to pressure	
3. in order to	
4. your values	
5. children and teenagers	
6. feel forced	
7. episodes of pressure	
8. a breakdown	
9. family ties	
10. too strong to break	

D Quels sont vos passe-temps ?

Français	Anglais	How to pronounce
la piscine	*the swimming pool*	la pea-seen
j'apprécie	*I like*	jah-pre-see
flâner	*to stroll or to saunter*	flan-nay
la montagne	*the mountain*	la mon-tahn
un bénévole	*a volunteer*	an bennay-vul
accueillir	*to welcome*	ah-coy-ear
soigner	*to care for*	swan-yay
l'occasion	*the opportunity*	low-caz-yon
de fil en aiguille	*gradually*	de feel on ay-gwee
maître	*master*	mett-re
cuisinier	*chef or cook*	cuiz-zeen-yay
une carrière	*a career*	oone car-ree-air
la saisonnalité	*the seasonality*	la say-zon-al-lee-tay

Écoutez maintenant Séverine, Nicole et Marc qui nous parlent de leurs passe-temps.

Severine
1. What sports does Séverine play?
2. What type of music does Séverine like in particular?
3. What is the name of the lead singer with Magma?
4. What else does Séverine like to do apart from sport and music?

Nicole
1. What does Nicole do every weekend?
2. Where did Nicole do voluntary work last year?
3. How many animals does the SPA welcome every year?
4. What does Nicole feel everyone can do for the SPA?
5. What type of help can you give the animal shelters?

Marc
1. What is Marc's favourite past-time?
2. Who is Marc's favourite chef?
3. What type of diploma would Marc like to do?
4. Give one example of how difficult the work of a chef is.

E La mode et le bal des débutantes

Français	Anglais	How to pronounce
les vêtements	clothes	lay vet-mon
les moqueries	teasing	lay mock-ker-ree
intégrer	to join / to fit in	an-tay-grey
un défilé de mode	a fashion show	an day-fill-lay de mode
maquillé(e)	made-up	mack-key-ay

Answer the questions below.

1. What is priceless in today's world?
2. What often happens to young people who cannot follow fashion?
3. What is the french for 'designer clothes'?
4. What has the Debs Ball become?
5. What type of pressure does the Debs put on girls?
6. How much can the Debs cost?
7. Why do some people not want to go to the Debs?

F Les sorties

Français	Anglais	How to pronounce
néanmoins	nevertheless	nay-on-mwah
coincé(e)	stuck	qwan-say
le danger	danger	le don-jer
la sécurité	security / safety	la say-cure-ree-tay
moche	ugly	mush

C'est important de partager des moments de bonheur. Nous allons écouter Jérémie, qui nous parle de sortir avec ses amis. Écrivez l'ordre dans lequel vous entendez les suivantes:

La phrase	Numéro
I don't go out more than that	1
Usually my mother brings me to town	2
I help at home	
Night-clubs are too expensive	3
After the pub's closing	
10 o'clock in the evening is considered early nowadays	
Considering the price of alcohol	4
Cities often have reputations for being dangerous	7
But this said	
It is really ugly	

G 1996 Leaving Cert Section III

Français	Anglais	How to pronounce
enfin	*finally*	on-fahn
les rapports	*relationships*	lay rah-pour
sous	*under*	sue
des troubles-fêtes	*spoilsports*	day troub-luh fett
plutôt	*rather*	plu-toe
les enquêtes	*surveys*	lays on-kett

You will now hear French sociologist Michel Fize being interviewed for a radio programme about young people today. The material will be played three times: first right through, then in four segments, with pauses and finally, right through again.

1. How, according to the speaker, have relationships between parents and teenagers changed between the sixties and the nineties?
2. According to the speaker, what above all do teenagers need in order to enjoy themselves?
3. What does the speaker say about newspapers?
4. What do all the surveys prove, according to the speaker?
5. What does the speaker say about young people's attitude to unemployment?

H Les faits divers

Français	Anglais	How to pronounce
comparaître	*to appear before*	com-par-ret
condamné à perpétuité	*sentenced to life*	con-dan-nay ah per-peh-chew-ee-tay
déraillement	*de-railment*	day-rye-mon
ladite	*the aforesaid*	la-deet
entretenir	*to maintain, to keep*	on-tret-ten-neer

Answer the questions below.

Article 1.
1. What age is the young man?
2. What sentence did he receive?

Article 2.
1. What happened to the train?
2. How many people were injured?

Article 3.
1. Who carried out this research?
2. By what percentage is one's chance of survival increased?

Oral Section – *Let's Get Talking*
Ten common questions asked on the subject of friends and friendship

Français	Anglais	How to pronounce
Décrivez votre meilleur(e) ami(e).	*Describe your best friend.*	day-cree-vay votr may-er amee.
Qu'est-ce que vous aimez faire le weekend ?	*What do you like to do at the weekend?*	kess-kuh vooz em-may fair le weekend?
Est-ce que vous allez partir en vacances après le bac ?	*Are you going on holidays after the leaving cert?*	esse-kuh vooz allay par-teer on vah-conce ah-pray le bac?
Avez-vous déjà visité la France ?	*Have you ever visited France?*	ah-vay voo de-jah viz-zee-tay la France?
Parlez-moi un peu de vos passe-temps ?	*Tell me about your pastimes.*	par-lay moi an puh de voh pass-ton
Est-ce que vous vous sentez sous pression de sortir avec les amis tous les weekends ?	*Do you feel under pressure to go out with friends every weekend?*	esse-kuh voo voo son-tay sue press-yon de sor-teer avec lays ah-mee too lay weekends?
Que pensez vous de la mode ?	*What do you think of fashion?*	kuh pon-say voo de la mode?
Parlez-moi de votre bal de débutantes.	*Tell me about your debs.*	par-lay moi de votr bal de deb-bue-tont
Que répresente l'amitié pour vous ?	*What does friendship mean to you?*	kuh re-pre-zont lam-mee-tee-ay poor voo?
Est-ce que la publicité met de la pression sur les épaules des jeunes ?	*Does advertising put pressure on the shoulders of young people?*	esse-kuh la pub-liss-see-tay may de la press-yon sewer lays ay-pole day jeun?

Dix questions et réponses possibles sur les amis et l'amitié

1. **Décrivez votre meilleur(e) ami(e).**
   Bon, pour commencer, mon meilleur ami est très gentil et tolérant. Il me comprend comme personne d'autre, et je peux lui faire complètement confiance. Il est sérieux à l'école et il fait attention aux profs, mais il a un côté coquin aussi. Je m'amuse tellement avec lui, quand nous sortons avec la bande. (Change this paragraph if your best friend is a girl, paying attention to the spelling of adjectives).
   Well to start with, my best friend is very kind and tolerant. He understands me like nobody else, and I can trust him completely. He is serious at school and pays attention to the teachers, but he has a cheeky side as well. I enjoy myself so much with him, when we are out with the gang.

2. **Qu'est-ce que vous aimez faire le weekend ?**

Normalement je ne fais pas grand chose car j'ai dois me consacrer aux études. Le vendredi soir dès que je rentre de l'école je révise un peu car je ne veux pas attendre le dimanche. Je regarde un peu la télévision et je me repose après une semaine fatiguante. Mes parents sortent le vendredi donc je dois garder les petits à la maison. Le samedi je donne un coup de main soit dans la maison soit dans le jardin. Ça depend. Si je ne suis pas fauché(e), c'est le samedi que je sors. Mes parents me donnent un peu d'argent, mais depuis que papa a perdu son emploi, c'est souvent difficile et je dois piocher dans mes économies, mais cet argent est ma bourse pour la vie à l'université, alors j'essaie de me freiner un peu. J'ai hâte de finir le bac afin de vraiment apprécier les weekends.

Usually I don't do much as I have to devote myself to my studies. On Friday evenings, as soon as I come home from school, I do a bit of revision because I do not want to wait until Sunday. I watch the TV a bit and I relax after a tiring week. My parents go out on on Fridays so I have to mind the little ones. On Saturdays, I help around the house or the garden. It depends. If I'm not broke, it's on Saturday that I'll go out. My parents give me a bit of money, but since dad lost his job, it is often difficult and I have to dip into my savings, but this money is my budget for life at university, so I try to take it easy. I can't wait to finish the leaving cert in order to really appreciate weekends.

3. **Est-ce que vous allez partir en vacances après le bac ?**

Je ne sais pas trop encore. J'espère trouver un boulot cet été. Je veux faire des économies pour la vie universitaire. J'aimerais bien partir mais comme d'habitude je suis sans un sou. Je ne veux pas enfiler des perles pendant les grandes vacances, donc on va voir. Je sais que les jeunes de mon âge aime bien partir à l'étranger pour faire la fête ensemble, mais je ne sais pas si je pourrai. Je ne peux pas demander aux parents car ils ont assez des factures à payer.

I don't really know yet. I hope to find a job this summer. I want to save for university life. I would love to go but as usual, I am broke. I don't want to sit around doing nothing during the holidays, so we will see. I know that young people of my age love going abroad to party together, but I don't know if I will be able to. I cannot ask my parents as they have enough bills to pay.

4. **Avez-vous déjà visité la France ?**

Oui, je suis allé(e) à plusieurs reprises avec ma famille. Nous avons visité la Bretagne, Paris et le sud. Mon coin préféré est la Bretagne. Les gens sont très chaleureux et je pense que nous avons les mêmes idées dans la vie. Ils savent s'amuser. Le paysage en France est vraiment à couper le souffle. La nourriture est un délice et les français sont très ouverts surtout si vous faites l'effort de parler leur langue.

Yes I have been to France several times with my family. We visited Brittany, Paris and the south. My favourite corner is Brittany. The people are very welcoming and I think that we have the same ideas in life. They know how to enjoy themselves. The scenery is breathtaking. The food is delicious and the French are very open especially if you make the effort to speak their language.

Non, malheureusement je n'ai jamais eu l'occasion de visitier la France, mais j'espère y aller un jour.

No, unfortunately I have never had the opportunity of visiting France, but I hope to go there one day.

Chapitre 2 Les amis et l'amitié

5. **Parlez-moi un peu de vos passe-temps?**
   C'est bien d'avoir des passe-temps. Au moins cela nous permet de vivre autre chose que l'école tous les jours! En ce qui concerne mes passe-temps, j'en ai un tas. Tout d'abord j'adore la musique et je peux passer des heures à l'écouter dans ma chambre. J'aime la lecture. Mon écrivain péféré est…Il/elle écrit des romans qui sont plein d'intrigue. J'aime aussi sortir avec mes amis. Je suis une vraie cinéphile. Je vais au cinéma tous les weekends. Je dois avouer que sans mes passe-temps, il m'aurait été très difficile de tenir le coup cette année.
   It is good to have a pastime. At the very least it allows us to experience something other than school every day. Concerning my pastimes, I have a pile of them. Firstly, I love music and I can spend hours listening to it in my room. I like reading. My favourite author is … He/she writes novels which are full of intrigue. I also like to go out with my friends. I am a real cinema lover. I go to the cinema every weekend. I must admit that without my pastimes, it would have been very difficult to survive this year.

6. **Est-ce que vous vous sentez sous pression de sortir avec les amis tous les weekends?**
   Non, pas vraiment. Je sors si j'en ai envie et si j'ai les moyens. Si je ne veux pas sortir je reste à la maison. Il y a bien entendu des jeunes qui sortent tous les weekends, mais cela n'est pas le cas pour la plupart de nous. J'aime bien sortir pour m'amuser mais j'aime bien rester au sein de la famille aussi.
   No not really. I go out if I feel like it and I can afford it. If I don't want to go out, I stay at home. There are, of course, young people who go out every weekend, but this is not the case for the majority of us. I really like to go out to enjoy myself, but I like to stay with my family also.

7. **Que pensez-vous de la mode?**
   Aujourd'hui, la mode et les marques sont très importantes pour certains jeunes. La mode est le signe qu'ils appartiennent à un groupe social particulier. Souvent les familles n'ont pas les moyens de payer pour les vêtements de mode. Je trouve que c'est ridicule d'essayer de suivre les goûts d'une industrie. Je préfère mon propre style. Je m'habille de façon décontractée et ça me botte!
   Today, fashion and labels are very important for some young people. Fashion is the sign that they belong to a particular social group. Often families cannot affort to pay for fashionable clothes. I think that it is ridiculous to try and follow the tastes of an industry. I prefer my own style. I dress casually and that suits me!

8. **Parlez-moi de votre bal de débutantes.**
   Le bal des débutantes est une étape importante dans la vie des jeunes. Ceci dit, le bal met trop de pression sur tout le monde mais sur les filles particulièrement. Les filles doivent être bronzées, coiffées, maquillées et très bien habillées. Les billets peuvent coûter les yeux de la tête, autour de €70 le billet. Pour les filles, la robe doit être vraiment élégante. En tout, la soirée peut revenir à plus de €700. Il y a toujours des filles et des garçons qui ne veulent pas y aller. Je me demande si cela est dû à la pression financière ou la pression des autres. La seule chose qui inquiéte les parents est la disponibilité de l'alcool et de la drogue. Les garçons n'ont pas grand-chose à faire pour le bal, louer un smoking, se raser, se laver et ça y est!
   The debs ball is a rite of passage in young people's lives. This said, the debs puts pressure on everyone but especially on girls. The girls have to be tanned, hair done, made-up and

very well dressed. The tickets can cost a fortune, around €70 a ticket. For the girls the dress must be really elegant. Counting everything, the evening can come to more than €700. There are always girls and boys who do not want to go. I wonder if this due to financial pressure or pressure from others. The only thing that worries the parents is the availability of alcohol and drugs. Boys don't have too much to do for the debs, hire a tux, shave, wash and that is it!

9. **Que représente l'amitié pour vous ?**

   L'amitié est très importante dans la vie. C'est bien de pouvoir partager vos soucis et vos moments de bonheur avec des amis.
   Friendship is very important in life. It is good to be able to share your worries and your happy times with friends.

10. **Est-ce que la publicité met de la pression sur les épaules des jeunes ?**

    La publicité est partout et c'est certain qu'elle est puissante. Par contre, je ne peux pas dire qu'elle met de la pression sur les épaules des jeunes. Les jeunes décident d'acheter ou non un produit. Cela dépend des moyens disponibles et pas vraiment du niveau de pression.
    Advertising is everywhere and it's certainly powerful. On the other hand I can't say that it puts pressure onto the shoulders of young people. They decide whether or not to buy a product. It depends on whether the means are available and not really on the level of pressure.

Le Vocabulaire Essentiel

Français	Anglais	How to pronounce
l'amitié	*friendship*	la-mee-tee-ay
en toute amitié	*out of friendship*	on toot ah-mee-tee-ay
un pot de l'amitié	*a friendly drink*	an poh de la-mee-tee-ay
se lier d'amitié avec	*to make friends with*	se lee-ay da-mee-tee-ay avek
se faire des amis	*to make friends*	se fair days ah-mee
un verre de l'amitié	*a toast to friendship*	an vair de lah-mee-tee-ay
savoir dire non	*to know how to say no*	sav-war deer noh
la pensée indépendente	*independent thought*	la pon-say an-day-pon-dont
une qualité admirable	*an admirable quality*	oone cal-lee-tay ad-meer-rab
la camaraderie	*friendship*	la cam-mar-ad-ree

la fraternité	*friendship*	la fra-ter-nee-tay
les réseaux sociaux	*social networks*	lay ray-zoh so-see-oh
un message anonyme	*an anonymous message*	an mess-saje an-no-neem
un blog	*a blog*	an blog
la menace	*the threat*	la men-nasse
l'intimidation	*intimidation*	lan-timmy-dass-yon
des insultes	*insults*	days an-soolt
le chantage	*blackmail*	le shon-taje
l'ostracisme	*ostracism*	loss-tra-seize-em
les outils virtuels	*virtual tools*	lays oo-tee ver-chew-el
sauvegarder	*to save*	sauf-gar-day
les données	*facts, data*	lay don-nay
être coupable de	*to be guilty of*	et-re koo-pab de
mater	*to spy on*	mat-tay
le vol d'identité	*identity theft*	le vul dee-don-tee-day
les harceleurs	*harrassers*	lay ar-sel-ler
être attentif à	*to be attentive to*	et-re ah-ton-teef ah
la prise de contact	*getting in contact*	la preeze de con-tact
la proie	*the prey or the victim*	la praw
repli sur soi	*going into oneself*	re-plea sur swah
les signes de l'harcèlement	*the signs of bullying*	lay seen de lar-sell-mon
l'angoisse	*anxiety*	lon-gwauss
la haine	*hatred*	la en
être branché(e)	*to be in style or stylish*	et-re bron-shay
être câblé(e)	*to be with it*	et-re cab-lay
dans le coup	*in the loop*	don le koo
être déconnecté(e)	*to be out of fashion*	et-re day-con-neck-tay
être démodé(e)	*to be out dated, old-fashioned*	et-re day-moh-day
être désuet(-ète)	*out-dated, old-fashioned*	et-re de-sue-ay, de-sue-et
en vogue	*fashionable*	on vogue
être incontournable	*to be inevitable*	et-re an-con-toor-nab
être indémodable	*that will never go out of fashion*	et-re an-de-moh-dab
avoir un look	*to have a look*	av-war an look
un plouc	*a culchie*	an plook
être prisé(e)	*prized, highly valued*	et-re pree-zay
ringard	*corny*	ran-gar
être stylé(e)	*to be stylish*	et-re stee-lay
avoir son heure de gloire	*to have its time*	av-war son er-de-glwar

avoir un air de déjà-vu	*to seem out of date*	av-war an air de day-jah voo
être dans l'air du temps	*to be of its time*	et-re don lair do ton
être une tarte à la crème	*slapstick*	et-re oon tart a la crem
le couturier	*fashion designer*	le koo-ture-ree-ay
le grand couturier	*a renowned fashion designer*	le gron koo-ture-ree-ay
le créateur/ la créatrice	*the creator*	le crey-ah-tur, la crey-ah-treece
le mannequin	*the model*	le man-kan
le modèle	*the model*	le mo-dell
le/la photographe	*the photographer*	le/la foto-graf
le top model	*the top model*	le top mo-dell
cartonner	*to be successful*	car-ton-nay
commencer	*to start*	com-mon-say
créer	*to create*	crey-ay
déclencher	*to cause*	day-clon-shay
démarrer	*to start up*	de-mar-ray
se démoder	*to go out of style*	se de-mo-day
diffuser	*to broadcast*	de-fuse-ay
envahir	*to invade*	on-vah-ear
le/la styliste	*the stylist*	le/la stee-list
adapter	*to adapt*	ah-dap-tay
adopter	*to adopt*	ah-dop-tay
amorcer	*to begin, set in motion*	ah-mor-say
s'approprier	*to appropriate*	sa-pro-pree-ay
apparaître	*to appear*	ah-par-ret
s'implanter	*to establish oneself*	sam-plon-tay
influencer	*to influence*	an-flu-on-say
introduire	*to introduce*	an-tro-dweer
inventer	*to invent*	an-von-tay
plébisciter	*to popularise*	ple-beh-sea-tay
se répandre	*to spread oneself*	se re-pond
la pression	*pressure*	la press-yon
les ados	*adolescents*	lays ah-doh
subir	*to be subjected to*	sue-beer
persuader	*to persuade*	per-swede-day
j'en suis persuadé	*I am convinced of it*	jon-swee per-swede-day
semble être	*seems to be*	som-bl et-re
un ami loyal	*a faithful friend*	an amee-loy-al
triste	*sad*	treest

Châpitre 2 Les amis et l'amitié

déprimé	*depressed*	de-pree-may
chambarder	*to turn upside down or to upset*	shom-bar-day
être dans le pétrin	*to be in a fix*	et-re don le pet-ran
prenez garde	*be careful*	pren-nay guard
maintes et maintes fois	*time and time again*	mant ay mant fwoy
prendre de bonnes décisions	*to make wise decisions*	prond de bun day-siz-yon
une situation désagréable	*a difficult situation*	oone sit-you-ass-yon days-ag-ree-abl
une poule mouillé	*a wimp*	oone pool mwee-ay
une moumoune	*a coward*	oone moo-moon
un air de confiance	*an air of confidence*	an air de con-fee-once
défends ce en quoi tu crois	*stand up for what you believe*	de-fon se on qwah too kwah
perdre son temps	*to waste one's time*	perd-son ton
le plus fiable	*the most reliable*	le plu fee-abl
une bonne affaire	*a good deal*	oone bun ah-fair
être néfaste pour la santé	*to be bad for one's health*	et-re nay-fast poor la sawn-tay
résister	*to resist*	re-zist-tay
tenir tête	*to resist*	ten-near tett
lâcher prise	*to lose one's grip*	lash-shay preeze
le respect	*respect*	le res-pay

Dix constructions clés sur les amis et l'amitié

1. **C'est incroyable d'imaginer que** = *it is unbelievable to imagine that*
   C'est incroyable d'imaginer que la plupart de jeunes renoncent aux passe-temps en terminale.
   It is unbelieveable to imagine that the majority of young people give up pastimes in sixth year.

2. **Prévenir** = *to prevent*
   Il faut essayer de prévenir les accidents du ski.
   We must try to prevent skiing accidents.

3. **Limiter les conséquences** = *limit the consequences*
   Remember the verb « Limiter » has to be correctly conjugated into the tense you wish to use. The exception to this rule is when you use a modal verb at the beginning of the sentence. The modal verb is conjugated and the second verb in the sentence is left in the infinitive.
   Elle a su limiter les conséquences avec un peu de diplomatie.
   She knew how to limit the consequences with a bit of diplomacy.

4. **En admettant qu'on puisse + verb in the infinitive** = *although admitting that we can ...*
   Même en admettant qu'on puisse changer son avis, je ne suis pas persuadé(e) que cela doit être le chemin à prendre.
   Even admitting that we can change our opinion, I am not convinced that this is the way to go.

5. **Il semble que** = *it seems that*
   Il semble que les jeunes filles suivent plus la mode que les garçons.
   It seems that young girls follow fashion more than guys.

6. **Je crains qu'on ne puisse pas** = *I fear that we will not be able to ...*
   (note the use of subjunctive)
   Je crains qu'on ne puisse pas continuer à jouer car le terrain est complètement inondé.
   I fear that we will not be able to continue playing because the pitch is completely flooded.

7. **Tout ce qui fait + noun or verb** = *all or everything that concerns*
   Tout ce qui fait avancer le schmilblick est une chose positive.
   Everything that concerns progressing to a solution is a positive thing.

8. **Mettre à disposition** = *to put at the disposal of*
   Remember that the verb mettre must be correctly conjugated into the tense required. Note the example given is in the Passé composé, so the verb mettre was correcly conjugated into this tense.
   Il a mis sa maison à la disposition de ses amis pendant les grandes vacances.
   He put his house at the disposal of his friends for the summer holidays.

9. **De la même façon que** = *in the same way as*
   Elle a consideré la situation de la même façon que sa copine.
   She considered the situation in the same way as her friend.

10. **On peut simplement + verb in the infinitive** = *we can simply*
    On peut essayer de trouver une solution ou on peut simplement écarter le problème.
    We can try to find a solution or we can simply brush the problem aside.

Dix expressions authentiques et ludiques

1. Faire ripaille = *to eat and drink well in a banquet-like setting*
2. Régler son compte (à quelqu'un) = *to get even*
3. Le mont-de-piété / Chez ma tante / Le clou = *pawn-brokers*
4. Passer au caviar / caviarder = *hide, suppress or censor*
5. Le fin du fin = *the best of the best*
6. Tout schuss = *quickly, immediately*
7. Un corbeau = *a whistle blower*
8. Crever de faim / avoir la dalle = *to be starving*
9. Une planche de salut / Trouver son salut dans... = *last chance saloon / using a way of escaping a serious problem or catastrophy*
10. Faire du ramdam = *make a fuss*

CHAPITRE 3
La maison et le quartier

A Comment est votre maison ?

Français	Anglais	How to pronounce
ma pièce préférée	my favourite room	ma pee-ess pref-fer-ray
un cinoche	a cinema (familiar)	an sin-nush
la banlieue	the suburbs	la bon-leue
un H.L.M.	a council house	an ash-el-em
un terrain	a pitch or a plot of land	an tair-ran
lambiner	to laze about	lom-bee-nay
flemmarder	to chill out	flem-mar-day
tranquille	quiet, relaxed	tron-keel
fiable	reliable	fee-abl
une maison jumelée	a semi-detached house	oone may-zon joom-lay

Listen to Rachel, Jean, Julie and Alain and fill in the grid.

Name	Type of Housing	Number of Bedrooms	Area where they live	Favourite Room
Rachel				
Jean				
Julie				
Alain				

B Les sans abris

Français	Anglais	How to pronounce
les sans abris	homeless	lay sans-ah-bree
un foyer d'accueil	a hostel or shelter	an foy-ay dak-coy
également	equally or also	ay-gal-mon
reconnaître	to recognise / admit	ray-cun-net-reh
un soutien	a support	an sue-tee-an

Bonne Chance !

Écoutez et remplissez les blancs.

Trop souvent, _____ nous parlons de personnes _____ domicile, nous pensons à _____ qui résident dans la _____ ou foyer d'accueil. Cependant, une personne est _____ comme sans-abri lorsqu'elle ne _____ trouver d'hébergement _____. Par exemple, un jeune quittant le domicile _____ et trouvant refuge chez un ami different tous les _____ est également considéré comme sans-abri. Bien que la _____ soit souvent la cause principale de _____, il est cependant important de reconnaître que beaucoup de personnes sans domicile _____ souvent de problèmes de santé mentale et autres besoins _____ un soutien à prendre en compte afin de garder un _____ à long terme.

C — Les quartiers chauds de Paris et les émeutes

Français	Anglais	How to pronounce
les émeutes	*riots*	lays ay-mut
les difficultés	*difficulties*	lay diffy-cull-tay
caractériser	*to be typical of*	car-ak-ter-ree-zay
un vivier à délinquance	*a breeding ground for delinquency*	an viv-vee-ay ah day-lan-konce
défavorisé	*disadvantaged*	day-fa-vor-ree-zay

Écoutez et répondez aux questions sur l'article.

1. Quand est-ce que les émeutes ont-t-elles commencé en France ?
2. La violence urbaine est liée avec 3 choses. Mentionnez une.
3. Les jeunes font quoi en générale dès qu'ils affrontent les forces de l'ordre ?
4. Quel quartier a une réputation pour la délinquance ?
5. D'où viennent ces émeutiers essentiellement ?

D   Des maisons détruites en Chine

Français	Anglais	How to pronounce
s'écrouler	to collapse	say-cru-lay
une réplique	an aftershock	oone ray-pleek
un séisme	an earthquake	an say-is-meh
grièvement	seriously	gree-ev-mon

Écoutez et répondez aux questions sur l'article

1. Combien de maisons se sont écroulées ?
2. Quand est-ce que cette catastrophe s'est passée ?
3. Combien de personnes ont été blessées ?

E   Les maisons écologiques

Français	Anglais	How to pronounce
sauter	to jump	so-tay
d'abord	firstly	da-boar
chaud	warm or hot	show
malléable	malleable	mal-lee-abl
l'humidité	humidity	loo-mid-dee-tay
les champignons	mushrooms	lay shom-peen-yon
les moisissures	mould	lay moise-zee-sewer

You will hear several points for and against living in a wooden ecological house. Write down any three that you can in the space provided.

No.	For or against living in a wooden ecological house
	For
1.	
2.	
3.	
	Against
1.	
2.	
3.	

48   Bonne Chance !

F Les lotissements fantômes

Français	Anglais	How to pronounce
les entrepreneurs	building contractors	lays on-tre-pren-nur
la moitié	half	la mwot-tee-ay
les investisseurs	investors	lays an-ves-tiss-sir
l'achèvement	the completion	la-shev-mon
carrément	completely	car-ray-mon
les égouts	the sewers	lays ay-goo

Écrivez l'expression en Français après avoir écouté le CD.

Anglais	Français
the accommodation crisis	
building sites	
without scruples	
due to the fact	
the completion of the work	
broken windows	
it is the responsibility of the government	
it is unbelievable	
the law	
protect innocent people	

G Leaving Cert Section III 2010

Français	Anglais	How to pronounce
les locataires	tenants	lay lock-ka-tair
le tapage nocturne	night-time racket	le tap-paje knock-toorne
déménager	to move house	de-men-nah-jay
le plancher	the floor	le plon-shay

You will now hear a telephone conversation between Louise and her friend, Éric.
The material will be played **three** times: first right through, then in **three segments** with pauses and finally right through again.

Section 1.

1. What is the good news that Louise tells Éric about?
2. What was the final straw for Louise?

Chapitre 3 La maison et le quartier

Section 2.
1. Why, according to Louise, will her life be more difficult in the future?
2. What does Louise say about the tram?

Section 3.
1. When exactly was the house built?
2. What does Louise say is worrying her?

H Leaving Cert Section I 2011

Français	Anglais	How to pronounce
être pollué	*to be polluted*	etr pol-you-ay
toujours	*always*	too-jure
puisque	*because*	pweece- keh
il y a trop de	*there is too much*	il-ee-ah-tro-de
loin de tout	*far from everything*	lwan-de-too

You will now hear an interview with three people, Sylvain, Roselyne and Émile.
You will hear the material three times: first right through, then in three segments with pauses and finally right through again.

Sylvain
1. Give **one** reason why Sylvain likes country life.

Roselyne
1. Why is Roselyne happier now? (Give **two** reasons)

Émile
1. Why does Émile dislike living in Strasbourg?

I Les faits divers

Français	Anglais	How to pronounce
un arrondissement	*a district*	an ar-ron-deece-mon
une travée	*a span*	oone tra-vay
un rez-de chaussée	*a ground floor*	an ray-de-show-say
l'ouragan	*hurricane or cyclone*	lure-ra-gong
l'association caritative	*charitable association*	la-so-see-ass-yon carry-ta-teev

Article 1.
1. Où se trouve la plus petite maison de Paris ?
2. Combien mesure la façade ?

Article 2.
1. En 1987, quel est le nom de l'ouragan qui a fait tant de dégâts ?
2. L'ouragan a tué combien de personnes ?

Article 3.
1. Qui a fondé Bâtiment du Coeur ?
2. L'association a construit combien de maisons ?

Oral Section – *Let's Get Talking*
Ten common questions on the subject of my house and my area

Français	Anglais	How to pronounce
Où est-ce que vous habitez ?	*Where do you live?*	oo esse-kuh vooz ah-beat-tay?
Parlez-moi un peu de votre maison.	*Tell me about your house.*	par-lay moi an puh de votr may-zon.
Décrivez votre chambre.	*Describe your bedroom.*	day-creev-vay votr shomb-re.
Parlez-moi un peu de votre quartier.	*Tell me about your area.*	par-lay moi an puh de votr car-tee-ay
Qu'est-ce qu'il y a à faire pour les jeunes près de chez vous ?	*What is there to do for young people near you?*	kess-kill ee-ah ah fair poor lay jeun pray de shay voo?
Préféreriez-vous habiter en ville ou à la campagne ?	*Would you prefer to live in the town or in the country?*	pre-fer-rer-ree-ay voo ah-beat-tay on veel oo a la cam-pan?
Qu'est-ce qu'il y a à faire pour les touristes chez vous ?	*What is there to do for tourists where you live?*	kess kill ee-ah ah fair poor lay toor-reest shay voo?
Quelle est votre pièce préférée et pourquoi ?	*What is your favourite room and why?*	kel ay votr pee-ess pre-fer-ray ay poor-kwah?
Où est-ce que vous habiteriez si vous gagniez au loto ?	*Where would you live if you won the lotto?*	oo esse-kuh vooz ah-beet-ter-yay see voo gan-yay oh loto?
Quels sont les problèmes qui existent dans votre quartier ?	*What problems are there in your area?*	kel sawn lay prob-lem key egg-zist don votr car-tee-ay?

Dix questions et réponses possibles sur votre maison et votre quartier

1. **Où est-ce que vous habitez ?**

   Comme j'habite en banlieue, j'ai plein d'amis dans le coin. C'est un endroit qui bouge. Tout est à côté. C'est un quartier bien desservi par les transports en commun. Il y a un grand centre commercial à dix minutes de chez moi, et je m'y rends souvent pour rencontrer des amis. Le voisinage est sympa et bien entretenu.
   As I live in the suburbs, I have a lot of friends nearby. It is an area which is full of life. Everything is nearby. The area has excellent transport facilities. There is a big shopping centre ten minutes from my house, and I go there a lot to meet up with friends. The neighbourhood is nice and well maintained.

   J'habite un petit patelin qui s'appelle … C'est un endroit très agréable car tout le monde se connaît. Eh bien j'ai toujours vécu ici donc la vie à la campagne est innée pour moi. J'ai tous mes amis qui habitent à deux pas de chez moi, et nous sortons ensemble presque tous les weekends.
   I live in a small village called … It is a lovely area as everyone knows each other. And anyway, I have always lived here so life in the country is natural for me. All my friends live close by and we go out almost every weekend.

2. **Parlez-moi un peu de votre maison.**

   Ma maison se trouve à la campagne. C'est une maison individuelle entourée d'arbres et de champs. C'est une maison confortable et spacieuse. Pour être franche, je ne m'intéresse pas plus que ça ! C'est une maison et voilà. Il y a quatre chambres, un salon, une salle à manger, une cuisine et deux salles de bains.
   My house is in the countryside. It is a detatched house surrounded by trees and fields. It is a comfortable and spacious house. To be honest, I am not that interested. It is just a house. There are four bedrooms, a sitting room, a dining room, a kitchen and two bathrooms.

   Ma maison se trouve en banlieue. C'est une maison jumelée. Heureusement, on s'entend très bien avec les voisins. (You then give the same information as above.)
   My house is in the suburbs. It is a semi-detached house. Fortunately, we get on very well with the neighbours.

3. **Décrivez votre chambre.**

   J'aime beaucoup ma chambre. Elle est grande et c'est mon espace privé. Je passe des heures dans ma chambre à écouter de la musique ou à faire des révisions. Il y a un lit, une armoire, des étagères et des posters sur les murs. Les rideaux sont [couleur] et il y a une moquette / du parquet. Personne n'a le droit d'y entrer sauf si je les invite. Mes parents me laissent tranquille car ils savent que je suis quelqu'un de fiable et que je ferai le nécessaire en ce qui concerne mon travail scolaire.
   I love my bedroom. It is big and it's my private place. I spend hours in my room listening to music or studying. There is a bed, a wardrobe, shelves and posters on the wall. The curtains are [colour] and there is a carpet / a wooden floor. Nobody is allowed to enter unless I invite them. My parents do not bother me because they know that I am reliable and that I will do everything I need to do concerning my school work.

4. **Parlez-moi un peu de votre quartier.**
Là où j'habite est un endroit qui est très bien desservi par les transports en commun. Il y a plein de choses à faire pour les jeunes. Nous avons des terrains où nous pouvons jouer au foot ou au hurling. Il y a un cinéma juste à côté et nous avons des magasins et un centre commercial à dix minutes de la maison.
Where I live is an area which is very well served by public transport. There are a lot of things for young people to do. We have pitches where we can play football or hurling. There is a cinema very near and we have shops and a shopping centre ten minutes from the house.

Mon quartier est vraiment dans la brousse. Il n'y a rien ! Si je veux sortir avec mes amis, je dois demander à mes parents de m'amener en voiture. Je m'ennuie à mourir ! La maison la plus proche est à vingt minutes de chez nous.
My area is really out in the sticks. There is nothing there. If I want to go out with my friends, I have to ask my parents to take me by car. I am bored to death. The nearest house is twenty minutes from our house.

5. **Qu'est-ce qu'il y a à faire pour les jeunes près de chez vous ?**
J'ai vraiment de la chance, car il y a tant à faire près de chez moi. On peut aller en ville faire du shopping ou rencontrer des amis pour papoter. On peut faire n'importe quel sport que nous voulons car nous avons un beau centre de loisirs. Il y a de jolies promenades et nous avons un lac où nous pouvons louer des barques. Il y a des boîtes de nuit en ville ainsi qu'un cinéma, un théâtre et des musées. J'adore simplement flâner en ville avec des potes, et de temps en temps nous faisons du ski nautique dans le lac.
I am really lucky because there is so much to do near me. We can go to town shopping or meet up with our friends for a natter. We can do whatever sport we want as we have a great leisure centre. There are lovely walks and we have a lake where we can hire small boats. There are night clubs in town as well as a cinema, a theatre and some museums. I simply love strolling around town with my friends, and from time to time, we go water-skiing in the lake.

6. **Préféreriez-vous habiter en ville ou à la campagne ?**
Personellement je préfère habiter en ville. Il y a beaucoup plus à faire et à voir. Je me sentirais isolé(e) à la campagne.
Personally I prefer to live in town. There is much more to do and to see. I would feel isolated out in the country.

Je préfère la vie campagnarde. J'adore me réveiller aux sons de la nature. Je n'aimerais pas la vie en ville avec les embouteillages et le bruit des moteurs.
I prefer the rustic life. I love to wake up to the sounds of nature. I would not like city life with traffic jams and the sounds of car engines.

7. **Qu'est-ce qu'il y a à faire pour les touristes chez vous ?**
   Il y a des touristes qui aiment bien visiter ma ville. Nous avons un beau château qui date du treizième siècle. Il y a un joli jardin public avec un petit lac. C'est un endroit agréable et accueillant. Il y a de belles plages à dix minutes du centre ville et un terrain de camping. Il y a aussi un petit port de pêche et des activités maritimes.
   There are tourists who love to visit my town. We have a lovely castle which dates back to the thirteenth century. There is a pretty park with a small lake. It is a pleasant and welcoming place. There are fabulous beaches ten minutes from the town centre and a campsite. There is also a small fishing port with maritime activities.

8. **Quelle est votre pièce préférée et pourquoi ?**
   J'aime bien le salon car je peux m'évader en regardant la télévision pendant des heures ou bouquiner. C'est une pièce bien éclairée qui donne sur le jardin.
   I really like the sitting room because I can escape for hours watching television or reading. It is a very bright room with a view of the garden.

9. **Où est-ce que vous habiteriez si vous gagniez au loto ?**
   Je ne sais pas si je partirais à l'étranger. J'aime bien la vie ici en Irlande et de toute façon j'ai mes amis et ma famille ici. Je pense que si j'avais la chance de gagner le pactole, je ferais construire une maison énorme avec une piscine chauffée et une grande salle de jeux. J'aurais des chambres pour les amis et j'aurais des bonnes pour faire le rangement et un cuisinier pour préparer tous les repas.
   I don't know if I would go abroad. I really like the life here in Ireland, and in any case, I have my friends and my family here. I think that if I was lucky enough to win the jackpot, I would have a huge house built with a heated swimming pool and a big games room. I would have bedrooms for my friends, and I would have housekeepers to tidy up and a chef to prepare all the meals.

10. **Quels sont les problèmes qui existent dans votre quartier ?**
    Il y a bien sûr des problèmes sociaux dans mon quartier et je crois que la drogue est le problème le plus sérieux. Les dealers essayent de cibler les jeunes avec des fausses promesses. Je ne veux pas commencer car on peut vite devenir toxicomane. En plus, la drogue est simplement trop dangereuse. Elle attaque le cerveau et très vite ceux qui prennent la drogue tombent dans le piège de la dépendance.
    There are of course social problems in my area and I believe that drugs are the most serious problem. Dealers try to target young people with false promises. I do not want to begin as you can quickly become an addict. On top of that drugs are simply too dangerous. They attack the brain, and very quickly those who take drugs fall into the trap of dependancy.

Le Vocabulaire Essentiel

Français	Anglais	How to pronounce
le toit	the roof	le twah
le volet	the shutter	le vol-lay
la porte d'entrée	the front door	la port don-tray
le jardin de devant	the front garden	le jar-dan de de-von
la barrière	the gate	la bar-ree-air
la boîte aux lettres	the letter box	la bwot oh lett-re
la fenêtre	the window	la fen-net-re
le garage	the garage	le ga-raj
la véranda	the veranda	la veh-ron-da
la terrasse	the patio	la tay-rass
le jardin de derrière	the back garden	le jar-dan de der-ree-air
la cheminée	the chimney	la shem-me-nay
le grenier	the attic	le gren-nee-ay
la chambre	the bedroom	la shomb-re
le bureau	the office	le bure-row
la salle de bains	the bathroom	la sal-de-ben
la salle à manger	the dining room	la sal-ah-mon-jay
le salon	the sitting room	le sal-on
le palier	the landing	le pal-lee-ay
la cuisine	the kitchen	la quee-zeen
la buanderie	the utility room	la boo-on-der-ree
les toilettes	the toilet	lay twa-let
l'escalier	the stairs	less-cal-lee-ay
le séjour	the sitting room	le say-jure
la cave	the basement	la cav
le sous-sol	the basement	le sue-sul
en haut	upstairs	on oh
en bas	downstairs	on ba
le quartier	the area	le car-tee-ay
la campagne	the countryside	la cam-pan
la banlieue	the suburbs	la ban-leuw
la cité	the ghetto	la sit-tay
la ville	the town / city	la veel
le village	the village	le vil-laje
la poste	the post office	la post
la banque	the bank	la bonk
le cinéma	the cinema	le sin-nay-ma

l'hôpital	the hospital	lop-pea-tal
le théâtre	theatre	le tay-at-re
l'hôtel de ville	the town hall	lo-tel de veel
la mairie	the town hall	la may-ree
l'église	the church	leg-leeze
la place	the square	la plass
l'office du tourisme	the tourist office	lof-feece de toor-riz-meh
le syndicat d'initiative	the tourist office	le san-dee-ka din-niss-sia-teeve
la station service	the petrol station	la stass-yon ser-veece
la gare	the train station	la gar
la gare routière	the bus station	la gar roo-tee-air
le commissariat de police	the police station	le com-miss-sar-ree-ah de po-leess
la piscine	the swimming pool	la pea-sseen
le musée	the museum	le muse-zay
la bibliothèque	the library	la bib-leo-teck
l'auberge de jeunesse	the youth hostel	low-burj de jun-ness
l'hôtel	the hotel	lo-tel
le jardin public	the park	le jar-dan pub-leak
le stade	the stadium	le stad
les espaces verts	green areas	lays es-pass vair
les embouteillages	traffic jams	lays om-boo-tay-aje
la qualité de vie	quality of life	la cal-lee-tay de vee
la nature	nature	la na-ture
tranquille	peaceful	tron-keel
bruyant	noisy	bree-on
les champs	fields	lay shon
les montagnes	mountains	lay mon-tan
les rivières	rivers	lay riv-vee-air
la plage	the beach	la plaje
un lotissement	an estate	an lot-tiss-mon
l'urbanisme	urbanism	lur-ban-neez-meh
l'architecture	architecture	lar-she-tek-ture
le dispositif	the plan of action	le diss-pos-zee-teef
faire la cuisine	to cook	fair la quiz-zeen
passer l'aspirateur	to hoover	pass-ay lass-pir-ra-ter
faire les courses	to do the shopping	fair lay coorse
faire le ménage	to do the housework	fair le men-naj
faire le jardinage	to do the gardening	fair le jar-dee-naje
faire la vaisselle	to do the washing-up	fair la vess-sell

repasser	*to iron*	*re-pass-ay*
aider à la maison	*to help at home*	*ay-day ah la may-zon*
donner un coup de main	*to give a hand*	*don-nay an coo de mah*
ranger la chambre	*to tidy the bedroom*	*ron-jay la shomb-re*
mettre la table	*to set the table*	*met-re la tabl*
débarrasser la table	*to clear the table*	*de-bar-rass-ay la tabl*
nettoyer	*to clean*	*ne-toy-ay*
tondre la pelouse	*to mow the lawn*	*tondr la pel-lose*
faire le linge	*to do the washing*	*fair le lange*
essuyer	*to wipe*	*ess-swee-ay*
polir	*to polish*	*pol-leer*
sortir les poubelles	*to put the bins out*	*sor-teer lay poo-bell*
les voisins	*the neighbours*	*lay vwas-an*
le voisinage	*the neighbourhood*	*le vwas-zee-naje*
passer le balai	*to sweep*	*pass-ay le bal-lay*
s'occuper de	*to take care of*	*so-coop-pay de*
trier	*to sort*	*tree-ay*
recycler	*to recycle*	*re-see-clay*
un pavillon	*a detached house*	*an pah-vee-on*
une maison jumelée	*a semi-detached house*	*oone may-zon joom-lay*
une maison mitoyenne	*a semi-detached house*	*oone may-zon mit-twi-en*
un studio	*a bed-sit*	*an stu-dio*
un appartement	*an apartment*	*an apart-mon*
un immeuble	*a block of flats*	*an ee-meubl*

Dix constructions clés sur la maison et le quartier

1. **Chercher à = *to try to***
   (Remember that the verb chercher usually means to look for something but when it is put with **à**, it means to try to do something. Also the verb must be put into the tense of the sentence that you are constructing.)
   Malgré le fait que le loyer ne soit pas payé le propriétaire cherche à trouver une solution avec la locataire.
   Despite the fact that the rent is not paid, the owner is trying to find a solution with the tenant.

2. **Leur but étant de = *their aim being to***
   Jeanne et Paul veulent venir à Paris, leur but étant de vivre à côté de l'université.
   Jeanne and Paul want to come to Paris, their aim being to live beside the university.

3. **Je suis de l'avis que = *I am of the opinion that***
   Je suis de l'avis que la vie à la campagne ne convient pas à tout le monde, mais je l'adore.
   I am of the opinion that life in the countryside does not suit everyone, but I love it.

4. **Noun or subject + permettre à** = to allow someone or something, followed by **noun + de (to do something).**
   La gentillesse de Mme Fourgon permet à sa fille de rester en contact avec ses amis en Angleterre.
   Mrs. Fourgon's kindness allows her daughter to remain in contact with her friends in England.

5. **Avoir pour but de** = *has an objective to*
   Ils ont pour but de changer le système car il ne fonctionne plus.
   Their objective is to change the system as it no longer works.

6. **Je n'y arrive pas à** = *I am not able to...*
   Je n'arrive pas à faire mes études dans le salon car mes frères regardent la télévision sans cesse.
   I am not able to do my study in the sitting room because my brothers are always watching the television.

7. **À travers le/la** = *through followed by a noun*
   La fille a regardé à travers la fenêtre.
   The girl looked through the window

8. **Savoir se tenir à carreau** = *To know how to behave oneself*
   (Remember that savoir is a modal verb and is always followed by a verb in the infinitive)
   Quand le père est à la maison, les enfants savent se tenir à carreau.
   When the father is at home, the children know how to behave themselves.

9. **Avoir des opinions partagées** = *to have mixed feelings or opinions*
   J'ai des opinions partagées sur ce sujet.
   I have mixed feelings on this subject.

10. **Travailler d'arrache-pied** = *to work flat out*
    Les filles dans mon école travaillent d'arrache-pied cette année.
    The girls in my school are working flat out this year.

Dix expressions authentiques et ludiques !

1. Une vérité de La Palice / Une lapalissade = *a truism*
2. Faire le point = *make an assessment*
3. Faire du gringue à quelqu'un = *to flirt with someone*
4. Être à la côte = *to be broke, penniless*
5. Entrer en lice = *to enter a competition, to take part in a debate, to throw one's hat in the ring*
6. Faire le matamore = *to show off, to be a smart alec, to brag*
7. Muet comme une carpe = *to be completely silent*
8. Tirer sa révérence = *to leave*
9. Des mesures draconiennes / une loi draconienne = *extremely severe measures or laws*
10. Mettre à l'index = *to blacklist*

CHAPITRE 4 — Le sport

Aural Section

A Les Jeux Olympiques

Français	Anglais	How to pronounce
être chargé de	to be responsible for	et-re shar-jay de
la célébration	the celebration	la sell-lay-brass-yun
le drapeau	the flag	le dra-po
la flamme olympique	the olympic flame	la flam oh-lamb-peek
ainsi que	as well as	ann-see-kuh
un défi	a challenge	an deaf-fee
le terrorisme	terrorism	le ter-rer-riz-meh
une occasion	an opportunity	oone oh-caz-yun
le monde	the world	le monde

Écoutez et puis remplissez les blancs.

Les Jeux Olympiques _____ ont lieu tous ____ quatres ans dans une _____ ville choisie par ___ comité. La ville _____ est chargée d'organiser et ___ trouver des _____ pour les Jeux Olympiques de _____ à ce qu'ils soient en _____ avec la _____ olympique. La célébration ____ Jeux _____ de nombreux rituels et de _____ comme le drapeau olympique et la flamme olympique, ainsi que les cérémonies d'ouverture et de _____. Les Jeux Olympiques sont _____ si importants que _____ chaque nation est représentée. Une _____ ampleur a généré de _____ défis comme le boycott, le _____, la corruption et le terrorisme. Les Jeux sont _____ une excellente occasion pour la ville hôte et son _____ de faire leur publicité au monde.

B Le sport sanguinaire

Français	Anglais	How to pronounce
le sport sanguinaire	blood sports	le spor sang-gwee-nair
naturel	natural	nat-tweur-rell
à la suite de	following	ah-la-sweet-de
dégoutant	disgusting	deh-gou-ton
lutter	to fight against	lutt-tay

1. In the opinion of the author, what is not very natural?
2. Since the dawn of time, what has man wanted?
3. Give two examples of cruel and unfair sports, according to the author.
4. What would the author do if he were Prime Minister?

C L'impartialité des arbitres

Français	Anglais	How to pronounce
un arbitre	a referee	an ar-beat-
impartiale	impartial	am-par-see-al
une épreuve	a test	oone ay-preuv
les critères	criteria	lay cree-tear

Écoutez cet article et écrivez en français les phrases suivantes:

Anglais	Français
a person who must be impartial	
a sporting event	
respect for the rules	
unfortunately	
they are human beings	
at an international level	
it is usually	
volunteers	
there is unheard-of stress	
in order to	

Bonne Chance!

D. Les sportifs – sont-ils trop payés ?

Français	Anglais	How to pronounce
considérable	*considerable*	con-sid-dare-rabl
une carrière	*a career*	oone car-ree-air
seulement	*only*	sul-mon
gâté	*spoilt*	gat-tay
s'entraîner	*to train*	son-tren-ay
l'agilité	*agility*	la-geel-lee-tay
être mérité	*to be deserved*	et-re mer-ree-tay

Écoutez les 3 jeunes qui parlent des sportifs et qui demandent s'ils sont trop bien payés.

Jean-Luc
1. Dans l'école de Jean-Luc quel est le sujet principal donc les garçons parlent ?
2. Qu'est-ce que Jean-Luc veut faire dans la vie ?

Patrick
1. Que pense Patrick des sportifs ?
2. Combien gagnent quelques joueurs professionels par semaine ?

Susan
1. Pour quelle raison selon Susan, les sportifs ont la tête enforcée dans la sable ?
2. Elle donne deux raisons pour lesquelles l'argent gagné est mérité. Donnez-en une.

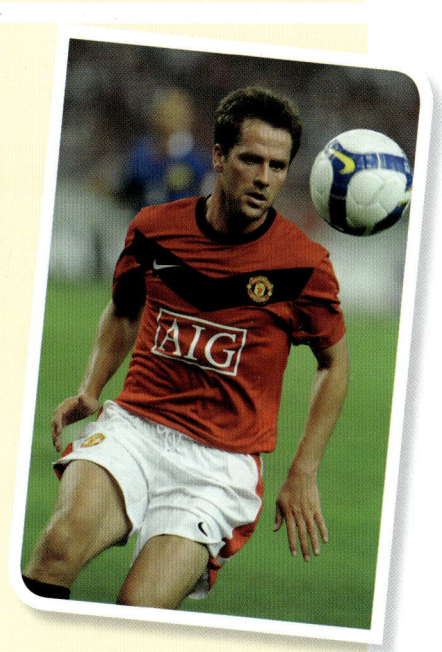

E. Le sport et la publicité d'alcool

Français	Anglais	How to pronounce
véritable	*true, or real*	vair-ree-tab-le
fidèle	*faithful*	fee-del
la publicité	*advertising*	la pub-liss-see-tay
pareil	*the same*	pah-rye
atteindre	*to reach*	ah-taand-re

Listen to the extract and indicate whether the following statements are true or false.

Statement	True	False
When children and teenagers become adults, they will remain faithful to the teams that they love		
Not everyone can understand that advertising is important		
Advertising companies use sport in order to reach the public		
Alcohol companies are not necessarily huge fans of these sports		
In 2002, the industry spent more than €586 million on alcohol advertisements		
They placed about 4,000 ads during sports programmes		
The government have started to do something before it is too late		

F Pourquoi les sportifs se dopent-ils ?

Français	Anglais	How to pronounce
améliorer	to improve	ah-mel-lee-ore-ray
l'effort	effort	lef-fore
récupérer	to recuperate	ray-coop-per-ray
répugnant	distasteful	reh-pun-yon

Marquez la phrase dans l'ordre dans lequel vous l'entendez.

Phrase	No
sporting people	1
recuperate	7
their aim is to	2
they take drugs	6
physical effort	4
it is distasteful	9
I am of the opinion that	8
to achieve this	5
the limits of their bodies	3
increase their stamina	3.5

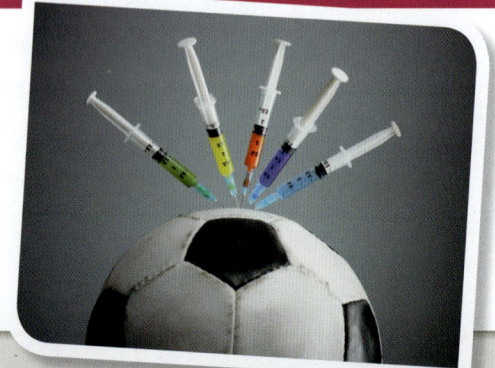

G. Leaving Cert 1998 Section I

Français	Anglais	How to pronounce
un cyclone	a cyclone	an see-clone
paralysé	paralyzed	para-lee-zay
les athlètes	the athletes	lays at-let
une medaille	a medal	oone meh-dye

You will now hear a radio interview with Claude Issora, a paralympic champion. The material will be played three times: first right through, then in three segments with pauses and finally, right through again.

1. What is Claude's handicap?
2. What event spurred Claude to begin training very seriously?
3. Write down two sources of income that Claude says he has.

H. Les faits divers

Français	Anglais	How to pronounce
le racisme	racism	le rah-seize-meh
se précipiter	to rush or to dash	suh press-sippy-tay
faillir	to almost do	fye-ear
s'apprêter à faire quelque chose	to get ready to do something	sa-pret-tay a fair kel-kuh shows
soupçonner	to suspect	soup-son-nay
radier	to strike off	rad-dee-ay

Écoutez et puis répondez aux questions.

Article 1.
1. Where did this incident take place?
2. How many people were watching at the time?

Article 2.
1. How many times had Lance Armstrong won the Tour de France cycling race?
2. The report on Lance Armstrong condemns three actions concerning performance-enhancing drugs. Name one of these actions.

Article 3.
1. What sport is mentioned in this news item?
2. Which country did the French team play in the semi-final?

Oral Section – *Let's Get Talking*

Ten common questions on the subject of sport

Français	Anglais	How to pronounce
Est-ce que vous faites du sport ?	*Do you play sport?*	esse-kuh voo fett do spor?
Qu'est-ce que vous faites comme sport ?	*What sports do you do?*	kess-kuh voo fett come spor?
Pourquoi est-ce que vous ne faites pas de sport ?	*Why do you not do any sport?*	poor-kwah esse-kuh voo ne fett pah de spor?
Quand est-ce que vous vous entraînez ?	*When do you train?*	kon esse-kuh voo vooz on-tren-ay?
À votre avis, pourquoi le sport est-il bénéfique pour les jeunes ?	*In your opinion, why is sport beneficial for young people?*	ah votr-avee, poor-kwah le sport et-teel bennay-feak poor lay jeun?
Est-ce que vous aimez regarder le sport à la télévision ?	*Do you like watching sport on television?*	Esse-kuh vooz em-may re-gar-day le spor ah la tellay-viz-yon?
Pourquoi est-ce que vous aimez ce sport ?	*Why do you like this sport?*	Poor-kwah esse-kuh vooz em-may se spor?
Est-ce que vous préférez les sports d'équipe ou individuels ?	*Do you prefer team sports or individual sports?*	Esse-kuh voo pre-fair-ray lay spor day-queep ou an-de-vid-du-el?
Qu'est-ce que vous pensez du dopage dans le sport ?	*What do you think of doping in sport?*	Kess-kuh voo pon-say do do-paje don le spor?
Quel rôle joue le sport dans votre vie ?	*What role does sport play in your life?*	Kel roll jew le spor don votr vee?

Dix questions et réponses possibles sur le sport

1. **Est-ce que vous faites du sport ?**

    Oui, je fais du sport. Je trouve que c'est une très bonne façon de rester en forme et de se faire des amis. Je joue au foot pour mon équipe locale et je m'entraîne trois fois par semaine. Si nous avons un championnat ou un match, il faut s'entraîner tous les soirs. Je me suis fait plein d'amis à travers le sport.
    Yes, I do sport. I find that it is a great way of staying in shape and making friends. I play football for my local team and I train three times a week. If we have a championship or a match, we have to train every evening. I have made a lot of friends through sport.

    Non, je ne fais pas de sport. Je suis un lecteur avide et je peux passer des heures à bouquiner. Je sais que le sport est bénéfique pour la santé, mais moi, je suis plutôt fainéant(e).

No, I don't do any sport. I am an avid reader and I can spend hours reading. I know that sport is good for your health, but I am rather lazy.

2. **Qu'est-ce que vous faites comme sports ?**
J'adore les sports d'équipe. Je joue au hockey / foot / basket / hurling / camogie / rugby / badminton. Je m'entraîne deux fois par semaine.
I love team sports. I play hockey / football / baketball / hurling / camogie / rugby / badminton. I train twice a week.

Je pratique un sport individuel. Je fais de l'athlétisme / de l'aviron / de l'escrime / de l'équitation / du cyclisme / du judo. J'adore pratiquer ce sport car c'est un bon moyen d'oublier les soucis de l'école.
I practice individual sport. I do athletics / rowing / fencing / horse-riding / cycling / judo. I love doing this sport because it is a good way of forgetting the worries of school.

3. **Pourquoi est-ce que vous ne faites pas de sport ?**
Je ne sais pas trop. Ce n'est pas mon truc c'est tout. J'aime bien regarder le sport à la télévision mais je me consacre à la musique. Je joue du piano et je n'ai pas le temps de faire autre chose, car un jour, je voudrais devenir pianiste d'orchestre.
I don't really know. It is not my thing that's all. I quite like watching sport on television but I devote myself to music. I play the piano and I do not have the time to do other things because, one day, I would like to become a concert pianist.

4. **Quand est-ce que vous vous entraînez ?**
Je m'entraîne tous les lundis et les jeudis. L'entraînement peut avoir lieu tous les soirs si nous avons un match. Notre entraîneur peut nous appeler le mardi pour être sur le terrain ce soir là et il faut obéir aux ordres sans discuter.
I train every Monday and Thursday. The training can take place every evening if we have a match. Our coach can call us on Tuesday to be on the pitch that particular evening and we have to obey orders without question!

5. **À votre avis, pourquoi le sport est-il bénéfique pour les jeunes ?**
À mon avis, le sport donne aux jeunes un équilibre dans la vie. Ça nous aide à développer un esprit d'équipe et d'apprendre le soutien entre amis. En plus, c'est bien de pouvoir partager des moments de bonheur et avoir le sentiment de faire partie de quelque chose.
In my opinion, sport gives young people balance in life. It helps us to develop a team spirit and to learn support among friends. On top of that, it is good to be able to share moments of happiness and to have the feeling of being part of something.

6. **Est-ce que vous aimez regarder le sport à la télévision ?**
Oui, j'aime bien regarder le sport à la télévision, surtout les championnats de haut niveau. En plus, c'est souvent le cas que je ne peux pas me deplacer pour assister directement aux matches, donc c'est beaucoup moins cher de suivre le sport à la télé.
Yes I really like watching sport on television, especially high-level championships. On top of that, it is often the case that I cannot travel to attend matches, so it is a lot less expensive to follow sport on tv.

7. **Pourquoi est-ce que vous aimez ce sport ?**
   Je m'intéresse à ce sport car cela demande beaucoup d'habilité et j'apprends énormément grâce à cette activité.
   I am interested in this sport because it requires a lot of skill and I am learning a great deal thanks to this activity.

8. **Est-ce que vous préférez les sports d'équipe ou individuels ?**
   Personellement, je préfère les sports d'équipe car il y a une très bonne ambiance entre joueurs et il y a toujours du soutien.
   Personally, I prefer team sports because there is a very good atmosphere between players and there is always support.

   Moi, je suis plutôt attiré(e) par les sports individuels. Je fais de l'athlétisme et malgré le fait que je sois membre d'un club, la pression est sur mes épaules le jour d'une course. Seulement ma performance personelle compte.
   Me, I am more attracted to individual sports. I do athletics and despite the fact that I am a member of a club, the pressure is on my shoulders the day of a race. Only my personal performance counts.

9. **Qu'est-ce que vous pensez du dopage dans le sport ?**
   Le dopage dans le sport est une triste réalité de nos jours. Je ne comprends pas pourquoi les gens veulent prendre des produits pour améliorer leurs performances. Je suis de l'avis que le dopage est quelque chose de malhonnête. Les sportifs essayent toujours de battre leurs propres records. C'est répugnant pour ceux qui essayent de gagner par leurs efforts, et pour le nom du sport.
   Doping in sport is a sad reality nowadays. I do not understand why people want to take products to improve their performance. I am of the opinion that doping is something dishonest. Sports people are always trying to beat their own records. It is repulsive for those who try to win by their own effort, and for the name of sport.

10. **Quel rôle joue le sport dans votre vie ?**
    Je trouve que le sport joue un rôle considérable dans ma vie. Pour moi, le sport est un moyen de se détendre. Il me permet de faire le vide et de me défouler. Je sais bien que l'exercise est très important, surtout quand on prépare le bac. Quand je fais du sport j'oublie mes soucis et la pression du bac.
    I find that sport plays a considerable role in my life. For me, sport is a way of relaxing. It allows me to let off steam and unwind. I know that exercise is very important, especially when we are preparing for the Leaving Cert. When I play sport, I forget my worries and the pressure of the Leaving Cert.

    Le sport ne joue pas un rôle important dans ma vie. Je suis tellement prise par d'autres moyens d'évasion comme la musique et les arts dramatiques. J'aime bien faire des promenades, mais ce n'est pas vraiment du sport proprement dit.
    Sport does not play an important role in my life. I am so taken up with other methods of escape such as music and acting. I quite like walking, but that is not strictly a sport.

Le Vocabulaire Essentiel

Français	Anglais	How to pronounce
battre un record	to beat a record	batr an rek-cor
classement officiel	official ranking	class-mon oh-fice-see-el
le tirage au sort	random selection	le teer-raj oh saur
le parcours	the course	le par-coor
le tenant du titre	the title holder	le ten-non do teetr
calendrier des épreuves	schedule of events	ka-lawn-dree-ay days ay-preuv
un formulaire d'inscription	an entry form	an for-mu-lair dan-scrips-yon
attendre la décision	to wait for the decision	ah-tondr la day-seez-yon
avertir	to warn	ah ver-teer
l'arrivée	the finishing line	lar-ree-vay
l'arbitrage	refereeing	lar-bee-traj
admission hors qualification	wild card entry	ad-miss-yon oar kali-fee-cass-yon
adversaire	opponent	ad-ver-sair
l'équité sportive	sporting fairness	lek-key-tay spor-teev
une décision annulée	a null decision	oone day-seez-yon an-ou-lay
la rencontre	the game / match	la ron-cont-re
une suspension	a suspension	oone sus-ponce-yon
l'impact direct sur le jeu	the direct impact on the game	lam-packed dee-rect sewer le juh
une infraction	an offense	oone an-frax-yon
avoir le dernier mot	to have the last word	av-war le der-nee-ay mo
en cas de litige	in case of dispute	on ka de li-tije
appliquer des sanctions	to apply sanctions	ah-pleek-kay day sanks-yon
une faute	a fault	oone phot
les lignes de touche	side lines	lay leen de tooch
le centre du terrain	the middle of the pitch	le centr do tear-ran
la régle du hors jeu	the off side rule	la regl do oar juh
le but en or	the golden goal	le boot on oar
accomplir	to accomplish	ah-kom-plear
un exploit extraordinaire	incredible exploits	an ex-ploi ex-tror-deen-air
galvauder un talent	to waste a talent	gal-voh-day an tal-lon
se vanter	to brag or boast	se von-tay
l'arbitrage vidéo	video umpireship	lar-bee-traj vid-day-oh
pointilleux	pernickety	pwan-tee-yuh
un concurrent mécontent	an unhappy player	an kon-coor-ron may con-ton

laisser son empreinte	to leave one's mark	less-ay son am-prant
faire rêver	to allow one to dream	fair re-vay
un coup de génie	a master stroke	an coo de jen-nee
établir un record	set a record	ay tab-lear an rek kor
remporter une médaille	to win a medal	rom-por-tay oone med-dye
conquérir	to conquer	kon-care-reer
briller	to shine	bree-ay
arriver en tête	to be first	ar-ree-vay on tet
un sportif de haut niveau	a high level sportsperson	an spor-tif de oh nee-voh
la diffusion des matchs	the transmission of matches	la de-fuse-yon day match
une prime	a bonus	oone preem
bien-loti(e)	well-off	bee-en lot-tee
mal-loti(e)	badly off	mal lot-tee
une blessure	an injury	Oone bless-your
une réussite éphémère	a fleeting success	Oone ray-oo-seat ef-fee-mare
la retraite	retirement	la reh-tret
remporter le championnat	to win the championship	rom-por-tay le shom-pee-on-nah
une carrière à courte durée	a short term career	oone car-ree-air ah koort doo-ray
offusquer	to offend	oh-fus-kay
toucher le pactole	to make a fortune	too-shay le pack-tul
l'excellence sportive	sporting excellence	lex-say-lonce spor-tive
au top mondial	at the top	oh top mon-dee-al
l'entraînement des sportifs	the training of sporting people	lon-tren-mon day spor-tif
le niveau sportif	sporting level	le nee-voh spor
la pression	pressure	la press-yon
l'esprit sportif	sporting spirit	less-pree spor-teef
un/une adepte	enthusiast	an/oone ah-dept
une adresse	a skill	oone ah-dress
se consacrer à	to devote oneself to	se con-sack-ray ah
eliminatoire	preliminary	el-lim-me-na-twar
l'équipement	equipment	lay-keep-mon
un événement sportif	a sporting event	an ev-ven-mon spor-teef
une étape	a stage	oone ay-tap
le dopage	doping	le do-paje
les produits dopants	doping products	lay pro-dwee dop-pon
une victoire	a victory	oone vik-twar
grimper	climb	gram-pay
l'exploit	the exploit	lex-ploi

réaliser	to achieve	ray-al-lee-zay
un entraînement acharné	relentless training	an on-tren-mon ah-shar-nay
s'attendre à	to expect to	sa-tondr ah
empêcher	to prevent	om-peh-shay
notamment	notably	note-ta-mon
c'est de la triche	it is cheating	say de la treech
des effets secondaires	side-effects	days ef-fay sek-con-dare
une prise de sang	a blood test	oone preeze de sang
les échantillons	samples	lays ay-shon-tee-on
viser	to target	vee-zay
le développement des capacités motrices	the development of motor skills	le dev-vel-up-mon day ka-pa-see-tay mo-treece
la pratique	the practice	la pra-teek
l'autonomie	autonomy	low-ton-oh-me
le soutien	support	le sue-tee-en
l'esprit d'équipe	team spirit	less-pree day-keep
se tenir comme des mollusques	to act like wimps	se ten-near com day mul-losk
un atout pour réussir	an asset to succeeding	an ah-too poor ray-oo-seer
promouvoir	promote	pro-moo-vwar
les vainqueurs	the winners	lay van-ker
un tremplin	a stepping stone	an trom-plan
faire le fier	to show off	fair le fee-air
un carton jaune	a yellow card	an car-ton jaune
le temps additionnel	extra time	le ton ad-diss-see-oh-nel
marquer un but	to score a goal	mar-kay an boo
un pénalty contestable	a questionable penalty	an pen-nal-tee con-tess-tabl
taper le ballon	to kick the ball	tap-pay le bal-lon
un carton rouge	a red card	an car-ton rooj

Dix constructions clés sur le sport

1. **Nul doute que = *nobody doubts that***
   Nul doute que les sportifs s'entraînent beaucoup afin d'améliorer leurs performances.
   Nobody doubts that sports people train a lot in order to improve their performance.

2. **Sans doute = *without doubt***
   Je partage l'avis exprimé ici que la pratique du dopage est sans doute contraire à l'esprit du sport.
   I share the opinion expressed here that the practice of doping is without doubt contrary to the spirit of sport.

3. **C'est une affaire d'opinion** = *it is an issue of opinion*
   Dans le sport, l'arbitrage vidéo est une affaire d'opinion avec ses partisans et ses adversaires.
   In sport, video umpireship is an issue of opinion with its supporters and opponents.

4. **Il faut que le gouvernement** = *the government should (or must) + verb in the subjunctive*
   Il faut que le gouvernement lutte contre cette pratique barbare.
   The government must fight against this barbaric practice.

5. **Vouloir faire comme** = *to copy or to do the same as someone*
   Il veut faire comme le mec à la télévision.
   He wants to do the same as the guy on the television.

6. **Se dérouler** = *to take place*
   (Note that this is a reflexive verb and must be conjugated with the verb être in the past tense)
   L'évènement s'est déroulé sans aucun incident.
   The event took place without incident.

7. **C'est l'occasion pour** = *someone or something + de + infinitive = it is the opportunity for someone or something to ...*
   Le championnat aura lieu la semaine prochaine et c'est l'occasion pour les joueurs de montrer leur talent.
   The championship will take place next week and it is the opportunity for the players to show their talent.

8. **Faire de son maximum** = *to do one's best*
   Souvent le sport est une carrière à courte durée donc, if faut faire de son maximum avec cette réussite éphémère.
   Often sport is a short term career so it is important to do one's best with this fleeting success.

9. **Détenir le record** = *to hold the record*
   Marie Pontique détient le record pour le cent mètres papillon en Australie.
   Marie Pontique holds the record for the hundred metre butterfly in Australia.

10. **Jouer un rôle considérable** = *to play an important role*
    Le sport joue un rôle considérable dans ma vie.
    Sport plays an important role in my life.

Dix expressions authentiques et ludiques

1. La dive bouteille = *the bottle of wine or the drink*
2. Tourner autour du pot = *to beat about the bush*
3. Attendre sous l'orme = *to wait a very long time in vain*
4. Vaincre / battre à plate(s) couture(s) = *to win a decisive victory*
5. Pour un point, Martin perdit son âne = *to lose something stupidly through negligence*
6. Appeler un chat un chat = *to call a spade a spade*
7. Une fine lame = *someone with a razor sharp intellect*
8. Un chevalier d'industrie = *a conman*
9. Ne pas valoir un clou = *to be worth nothing, valueless*
10. Être dans ses petits souliers = *to feel uncomfortable*

Chapitre 5 L'économie

Aural Section

A Les petits boulots

Français	Anglais	How to pronounce
les petits boulots	part-time jobs	lay pet-tee boo-low
résumer	to summarise	rez-zoo-may
l'adolescence	adolescence	lad-doh-ley-sonce
réel	real	ray-el
financière	financial	fee-non-see-air
même	even, self, same	mem
être embauché(e)	to be employed	et-ruh om-boh-shay
merveille	a marvel	mer-vay
des fringues	clothes (slang)	frang

Rémplissez les blancs

Normalement les petits boulots ne sont pas _____ par des contrats, mais parfois, ceux qui ____ des petits boulots ont un contrat de travail à _____ déterminée. Pour résumer, on peut _____ que l'accès au monde du travail constitue une _____ importante durant l'adolescence. Il _____ un premier contact réel avec le _____ de l'entreprise. C'est à ce _____ aussi que l'on apprend à gérer l'argent gagné par ses propres _____, pour accéder ainsi à un début d'autonomie _____. En France les mineurs ont besoin de l'autorisation de leur parents pour les _____ boulots, même pour les _____ d'été. L'employeur doit leur demander une autorisation, obligatoire pour les _____ de 16 ans.

Name	Where does or did this person work?	What type of work do they or did they do?	What is their opinion of their work?
Dominic			
Émilie			
Stéphane			

B Le tigre celtique !

Français	Anglais	How to pronounce
les immigrés	*immigrants*	lays im-me-grey
surtout	*especially*	soor-too
chaleureux	*warm, welcoming*	shal-lur-ruh

Listen to the article and find the French words for the following:

English	French
the hopes of a people	
such a short time ago	
a shortage of man power	
eastern countries	
incredibly racist	
the Irish changed overnight	
the cult of banking	
top of the range cars	
exotic	
the skullduggery	

C La main d'œuvre enfantine

Français	Anglais	How to pronounce
le phenomène	*the phenomenon*	le fen-no-men
l'occident	*the west*	locks-see-don
en voie de	*on the road to, in the process of*	on vawe de
prospérité	*prosperity*	pross-per-ee-tay
illettrisme	*illiteracy*	ee-leh-treesm
en dépit de	*in spite of*	on dep-pea duh

Bonne Chance !

Listen to the following article on child labour and write the order in which the phrases given were mentioned:

Statement	Number
the phenomenon of child labour exists	
there are laws which protect children	
leads to poverty, debt, illiteracy and the absence of social protection	
western people want to buy cheaper and cheaper products	
children must work non-stop	
subsistence of their families	
it is incredible nowadays	
to achieve this	
child labour is a sad fact in the world	
in order to	

D La chute bancaire

Français	Anglais	How to pronounce
la racine	*the root*	la rah-scene
à l'époque	*at the time, during the era*	ah lay-pock
manger à tous les râteliers	*to have a finger in every pie*	mon-jay ah too lay rah-tell-yay
plusieurs	*several*	plooze-zee-er
les citoyens	*citizens*	lay sit-y-en

Citez l'ordre dans lequel vous entendez les phrases suivantes:

Phrase	Numéro
the debt crisis in Greece	
for the last number of years	
life is not like that	
bankers wanted to have a finger in every pie	
investors fear	
too many people wanted to become too rich too quickly	
as a consequence of this	
under enormous pressure	
it is up to the government	
greed is really the root of the banking collapse in Ireland	

Chapitre 5 L'économie

Écoutez cet extrait et répondez aux questions suivantes:

1. Quelle est la cause principale de la chute bancaire?
2. Qu'est-ce que ça veut dire «chercher des noises»?
3. Les investisseurs ont peur de quoi exactement?
4. Qu'est-ce que le gouvernement doit faire?

E Le chômage

Français	Anglais	How to pronounce
les événements	events	lays ay-ven-mon
le taux	the rate	le taw
les allocations familiales	child benefit	lays al-low-cass-yon fa-mil-lee-al
etre êmbauché	to be hired or employed	etr om-boh-shay
les initiatives	initiatives	lays in-niss-see-ah-tiv
depuis	for / since	de-pwee
l'ère	the era	layer

Tous les blancs sont des verbes! Essayez d'en trouver et puis écoutez pour voir si vous avez réussi.

Les événements en Irlande _____ une tournure tragique. Le taux de chômage ____ en hausse. Actuellement presque quatorze pour cent de la population active ____ sans emploi. La situation ne _____ pas de _____. Le nombre de demandeurs d'emploi qui _____ les allocations familiales ____ également en augmentation. Il _____ au gouvernement de _____ quelque chose avant qu'il ne ___ trop tard. L'état __ déjà _____ un tas d'initiatives qui _____ eventuellement ____ ceux qui ____ ____ par la misère. Les jeunes diplômés _____ à l'étranger à la recherche d'un boulot stable. L'Irlande __ beaucoup _____ depuis l'ère du tigre celtique.

F Les compagnies aériennes à bas prix

Français	Anglais	How to pronounce
une compagnie	a company	oone com-pah-nee
un appareil	an instument, machine or aircraft	ann ah-pah-rye
réaliser	to achieve or attain	ray-ah-lee-zay
l'entretien	upkeep or maintenance	lon-tre-tien
déçu(e)	disappointed	day-sue

Écoutez et puis répondez aux questions :

1. Il y a combien de compagnies low cost dans le monde actuellement ?
2. En quelle année, la première compagnie a-t-elle été inventée ?
3. La flotte de Ryanair est composée de quel type d'appareil ?
4. Où est le siège de Ryanair ?
5. En quelle année la compagnie Ryanair a-t-elle été crée et par qui ?
6. Qui a lancé Transavia ?
7. Dans quelles circonstances est-il difficile de communiquer avec Ryanair ?

G   Leaving Cert 2011 Section II

Français	Anglais	How to pronounce
un apprentissage	*an apprenticeship*	an ah-pron-tee-saje
coiffeur	*hair-dresser*	kwauf-fer
un entretien	*an interview*	an on-tre-tjan
être embauché	*to be hired or employed*	etr om-boh-shay
les collègues	*colleagues*	lay col-egg
paresseux	*lazy*	par-reh-suh

You will now hear a young man, Jérémy, talking about his job. The material will be played three times: first right through, then in four segments with pauses, and finally right through again.

1. Mention one job which Jérémy has had in the past.
2. Jérémy had a problem finding a job because he didn't speak
    (a) Spanish
    (b) English
    (c) German
    (d) Italian
3. How did Jérémy hear about a possible job?
    (a) By phone
    (b) By text message
    (c) By letter
    (d) By e-mail
4. Give one thing that Jérémy's new boss is saying about him.

Chapitre 5 L'économie

H Les faits divers

Français	Anglais	How to pronounce
l'occasion	*the opportunity*	low-caz-yon
un éventail	*a fan or a range*	an ev-von-tye
ambitieux	*ambitious*	om-biss-yuh
souligner	*to emphasise*	soo-leen-yeh
les cheminots	*railway workers*	lay chim-mee-no
un renfort	*reinforcement / backup*	an ron-four

Article 1.
1. Where and when is the Trade Fair opening?
2. Who will be exhibiting at the Trade Fair?

Article 2.
1. Name one point President Chirac makes about the car industry.

Article 3.
1. What was the cause of this strike?
2. What have the strikers been promised?

Oral Section – *Let's Get Talking*

Ten common questions on the subject of the economy

Français	Anglais	How to pronounce
Est-ce que vous recevez de l'argent de poche ?	*Do you receive pocket money?*	esse-kuh voo re-cev-vay de lar-jon de posh?
Comment dépensez-vous votre argent ?	*How do you spend your money?*	come-on day-pon-say voo votr ar-jon?
Avez-vous un petit boulot cette année ?	*Have you a part-time job this year?*	ah-vay voo an pet-tee boo-lo set an-nay?
Qu'est-ce que vous faites pour gagner de l'argent ?	*What do you do to earn money?*	kes-kuh voo fett poor gan-yay de lar-jon?
Est-ce que vous pensez que c'est une bonne idée d'avoir un petit boulot en terminale ?	*Do you think that it is a good idea to have a part-time job in 6th year?*	esse-kuh voo pon-say kuh sayt oone bun ee-day dav-war an pet-tee boo-lo on ter-mee-nal?

Bonne Chance !

Où est-ce que vous travaillez ?	*Where do you work?*	oo esse-kuh voo tra-vye-ay?
Est-ce que vos parents exigent que vous donniez un coup de main à la maison ?	*Do your parents expect you to give a hand at home?*	esse-kuh vo par-ron egg-zeege kuh voo don-nay an coo de man a la may-zon?
Qu'est-ce que vous faites à la maison pour aider vos parents ?	*What do you do at home to help your parents?*	kess-kuh voo fett a la may-zon poor ay-day vo par-ron?
Combien est-ce que vous recevez chaque semaine ?	*How much do you receive every week?*	com-bee-en esse-kuh voo re-cev-vay shack se-men?
Est-ce que vous arrivez à faire des économies ?	*Do you manage to save?*	esse-kuh vooz arr-ree-vay a fair days ay-con-no-mee?

Dix questions et réponses possibles sur l'économie

1. **Est-ce que vous recevez de l'argent de poche ?**
   Non, je ne reçois pas de l'argent de poche. Je dois donner un coup de main à la maison comme presque tous les jeunes de mon âge, mais je ne reçois pas un sou. Je garde des enfants pour des voisins et je gagne un peu d'argent en faisant cela. Je n'ai pas à me plaindre car j'ai de la chance de pouvoir travailler un peu.
   No I don't receive pocket money. I must give a hand at home like most young people of my age, but I don't get a penny. I mind children for the neighbours and I earn a bit of money doing this. I can't complain as I am lucky to be able to work a little.

   Oui, je reçois €30 par semaine, mais il faut que j'utilise cet argent pour acheter quelque chose à manger à la cantine tous les jours. Si je veux sortir, il faut que je fasse un peu de ménage à la maison. Cela me dérange pas trop mais des fois, j'en ai ras-le-bol.
   Yes, I receive €30 a week, but I have to use this money to buy something to eat in the canteen every day. If I want to go out, I have to do a bit of housework at home. This does not bother me too much, but sometimes I get fed up.

2. **Comment dépensez-vous votre argent ?**
   Bon, d'abord j'achète des fringues et je fais des économies. Avec l'argent économisé je sors une fois par mois. Les sorties peuvent revenir très chère, mais cela vaut le coup car on s'amuse tellement.
   Well firstly I buy clothes and I save. With the saved money, I go out once a month. Nights out can be expensive but they are worth it because we enjoy ourselves so much.

3. **Avez-vous un petit boulot cette année ?**
   J'ai un petit boulot cette année. Je travaille à temps partiel dans un hôtel près de chez moi. Je travaille à la réception. Comme j'habite un endroit touristique, il y a toujours du travail pour les jeunes en été. Le travail est intéressant et en plus, je peux pratiquer mon français car nous avons pas mal des visiteurs français. J'adore mon travail.
   I have a job this year. I work part-time in a hotel near my house. As I live in a touristic area, there is always work for young people in the summer. The work is interesting and on top of that, I can practice my French as we have quite a lot of French visitors. I love my work.

Vu la situation actuelle en Irlande, ce n'est pas surprenant que je n'ai pas trouvé de travail cette année. L'année dernière j'ai travaillé à la caisse dans un supermarché près de chez moi. Le travail était facile et les heures me convenaient à merveille. J'ai travaillé surtout le weekend et pendant les grandes vacances. J'ai reçu €8 euro de l'heure et ce n'était pas mal.

Considering the current situation in Ireland, it is not surprising that I have not found a job this year. Last year I worked at the checkout in a supermarket near my home. The work was easy and the hours suited me wonderfully. I worked mostly at weekends and during the summer holidays. I earned €8 an hour and that wasn't bad.

4. **Qu'est-ce que vous faites pour gagner de l'argent ?**

   Je donne un coup de main à la maison et je garde les enfants de ma tante. Je tonds la pelouse pour mon père et je lave la voiture de ma mère. Je fais un peu de tout. Je m'occupe de mon frère et je prépare le repas tous les soirs.

   I give a hand at home and I mind my aunt's children. I mow the lawn for my father and I wash my mother's car. I do a bit of everything. I take care of my brother and I prepare the meal every evening.

5. **Est-ce que vous pensez que c'est une bonne idée d'avoir un petit boulot en terminale ?**

   Ça dépend. Si vous avez un petit boulot le vendredi soir ou le samedi, ça peut être faisable, mais il y a des jeunes qui travaillent tous les soirs et le weekend. Le travail scolaire souffre car ces jeunes sont trop fatigués. Je pense que c'est mieux d'attendre et de se consacrer aux études.

   It depends. If you have a job on Friday evenings or Saturday, it might be feasible, but there are young people who work every evening and weekends. School work suffers because these young people are too tired. I think that it is better to wait and to devote oneself to study.

6. **Où est-ce que vous travaillez ?**

   Je travaille dans un supermarché près de chez moi. Je travaille dans un restaurant. Je travaille dans un hôtel. Je travaille dans un magasin en ville. Je travaille dans une station-service.

   I work in a supermarket near my house. I work in a restaurant. I work in a hotel. I work in a shop in town. I work in a petrol station.

7. **Est-ce que vos parents exigent que vous donniez un coup de main à la maison ?**

   Oui, mes parents veulent que je fasse un peu à la maison. Ils ne sont pas trop stricts mais ils comptent sur moi. Je fais du rangement et je passe l'aspirateur car pour ma mère cette tâche est une vraie corvée.

   Yes, my parents want me to do a bit at home. They are not very strict but they count on me. I do general tidying and I do the hoovering because for my mother, this task is sheer drudgery.

   Non, c'est ma mère qui fait tout à la maison. Des fois, j'ai l'impression qu'elle est fatiguée mais j'ai l'habitude de rien faire. Je ne sais même pas comment fonctionne la machine à laver. Mes amis disent que je suis pourri gâté !

   No, it is my mother who does everything at home. Sometimes I have the impression that she is tired but I am used to doing nothing. I don't even know how the washing machine works. My friends say that I am spoiled rotten!

8. **Qu'est-ce que vous faites à la maison pour aider vos parents?**
   Je range les chambres et le salon. Je nettoie le frigo. Je sors les poubelles. Je tonds la pelouse. Je fais la cuisine. Je mets la table. Je vide la lave-vaisselle.
   I tidy the bedrooms and the sitting room. I clean the fridge. I put out the bins. I mow the lawn. I do the cooking. I set the table. I empty the dish-washer.

9. **Combien est-ce que vous recevez chaque semaine?**
   Je reçois à peu près €30 par semaine. Ça dépend si je sors ou pas. Souvent mes parents ne me donnent rien et de toute façon je ne veux pas les taxer car la vie est dure.
   I receive about €30 a week. It depends if I am going out or not. Often my parents give me nothing and anyway, I don't want to sponge off them because life is hard.

10. **Est-ce que vous arrivez à faire des économies?**
    Oui, j'économise €10 par semaine. Je les mets directement dans mon compte d'épargne à la banque.
    Yes, I save €10 a week. I put it into my savings account at the bank straight away.

    Non, l'argent me brûle les doigts. Je le dépense plus vite que je ne le reçois. J'aimerais bien pouvoir faire des économies mais je ne suis pas du tout discipliné(e).
    No, money burns a hole in my pocket. I spend it faster than I get it. I would love to be able to save, but I am not at all disciplined.

Le Vocabulaire Essentiel

Français	Anglais	How to pronounce
renouveler	to renew	re-new-vlay
travailler à temps-partiel	to work part-time	tra-vye-ay ah ton-par-see-el
le contrat de travail	the work contract	le con-tra de tra-vye
le fonctionnement de l'entreprise	the workings of the company	le fung-see-on-mon de lon-tre-preez
connaître ses droits	to know one's rights	cun-netr say dwah
l'apprentissage	apprenticeship	la-pron-tee-saje
résilier	to terminate (a contract)	re-zil-lee-ay
les conditions de travail	working conditions	lay con-diss-yon de tra-vye
les heures supplémentaires	overtime	lays er soup-le-mon-tair
un jour de congé	a day off	an jur de con-jay
les services juridiques	legal services	lay sir-veece jur-ree-deek
une période de forte croissance	a time of strong growth	oone per-ree-od de fort crwah-sonce
l'économiste	the economist	lay-con-no-meest
le niveau de vie	the standard of life	le nee-voh de vee

les impôts	*taxes*	lays am-poh
la capacité de production	*the capacity for production*	la ca-pass-see-tay de pro-ducks-yon
anglophone	*English-speaking*	ang-lo-fone
la stabilité	*stability*	la sta-bil-lee-tay
la création des emplois	*job creation*	la cray-ass-yon days aum-plau
la consommation des ménages	*household consumption*	la con-so-mass-yon day men-naje
la main d'œuvre enfantine	*child labour*	la man-dov-re on-fon-teen
le tiers monde	*the third world*	le tee-air mond
une mauvaise récolte	*a bad harvest*	oone mo-vaze re-cult
un aléa	*a hazard or a risk*	an ah-leh-ah
la faillite	*the collapse*	la fye-eat
souffrir de la faim	*to suffer from hunger*	soof-reer de la fan
la servitude des enfants	*the slavery of children*	la ser-vee-tood days on-fon
la survie	*survival*	la sir-vee
osciller	*to fluctuate*	oh-see-lay
constituer	*to make up*	con-stit-chew-ay
la prospérité	*prosperity, wealth*	la pross-per-ree-tay
la bourse	*the stock exchange*	la burse
dans le collimateur de	*under the scrutiny of*	don de coll-lee-ma-ter de
la dégringolade	*the collapse or the slump*	la day-grang-go-laad
la solvabilité	*solvency*	la sol-va-bill-lee-tay
en parallèle	*at the same time*	on para-lell
épargner	*to save*	ay-par-neay
le secteur bancaire	*the banking sector*	le sek-tur bon-care
un défaut	*a default*	an day-foh
les appels au calme	*call for calm*	lays ap-pel oh calm
le marché	*the market*	le mar-shay
le commerce équitable	*fair trade*	le com-merce ay-key-tab
le fournisseur	*the manufacturer*	le foor-nee-sir
les prix	*prices*	lay pree
étaler vos produits	*to exhibit your products*	ay-tal-lay voh pro-dwee
du conseil	*advice*	do con-say
à court terme	*short-term*	ah coor term
une hausse de chiffre d'affaire	*an increase in profits*	oone oas de sheaf-re daff-air
le client	*the client / customer*	le klee-on

la réussite	success	la ray-ou-seat
à bas prix	low cost	ah bah pree
les tarifs	the prices	lay tar-reef
les coûts	the costs	lay koo
les passagers	passengers	lay pah-sa-jay
une maximisation	a maximisation	oone maxi-miz-zass-yon
applicable	applicable	ah-plee-cab
une vague	a wave	oone vag
essaimer	to spread	ess-sem-may
à bord	on board	ah bor
un prix dérisoire	a derisory price	an pree der-riz-war
des spéculateurs	speculators	day spek-ta-ter
puiser	to draw on	pwee-zay
tomber dans le rouge	to go into the red	tom-bay don le rouge
l'incertitude	incertitude	lan-sir-tee-tood
la dette	debt	la dett
le plancher	rock bottom	le plon-shay
un taux	a rate	an tow
les pays endettés	countries in debt	lay pay-ee on-det-tay
déposer	to deposit	day-po-zay
les investisseurs	investors	lays an-ves-tiss-sir
le rendement	the productivity	le rond-mon
le comité d'enquête	the committee of enquiry	le com-me-tay don-quett
l'efficacité	efficiency	leffy-cass-see-tay
la dette souveraine	sovereign debt	la dett sue-ver-ren
la stabilité financière	financial stability	la sta-bill-lee-tay fee-nonce-see-air
l'économie irlandaise	the Irish economy	lay-con-oh-mee ear-lon-days
la bulle immobilière	the property bubble	la boul ee-mo-bill-lee-air
l'accélération des salaires	the growth of salaries	lack-sell-ler-rass-yon day sal-lair
la dette publique	the public debt	la dett pub-leek
le soutien financier	financial support	le sue-tee-en fee-nonce-see-air
une garantie	a guarantee	oone gar-ron-tee
l'escroqerie	deception	less-crock-ker-ree
endommager	to damage	on-doh-ma-jay
correspondre	to correspond to	cor-ress-pond
en raison de	because of	on ray-zon de

Chapitre 5 L'économie

être confronté par	to be confronted by	et con-fron-tay par
un acquéreur	a buyer	an ah-care-rer
voire	even	vwar
sembler	to seem to	som-blay
le commerce en ligne	online trading	le com-merce on leen
l'arnaque	swindle	lar-nack
se faire rembourser	to get a refund	se fair rom-boor-say
avoir recours à	to resort to	av-war re-coor ah
une rupture de stock	out of stock	oone rup-ture de stock
une commande	an order	oone com-mond
annuler	to cancel	an-you-lay
effectuer un achat	to carry out a purchase	ay-feck-chew-ay an ah-shah
le paiement en ligne	on-line payment	le pay-mon on leen
réaliser	to carry out	ray-al-lee-zay
une transaction	a transaction	oone tron-zaks-yon

Dix constructions clés sur l'économie

1. **Je trouve que = *I find that***
   Je trouve que la crise économique était provoquée par l'avarice des gens.
   I think that the economic crisis was caused by the greed of people.

2. **Noun + nous donne l'occasion de + infinitive = *gives the opportunity to***
   Le commerce en ligne nous donne l'occasion d'acheter des produits de chez nous.
   E-commerce gives us the opportunity to buy products from home.

3. **Par contre = *however, on the other hand***
   Ma mère trouve que les cartes à puce sont meilleures que les anciennes cartes de crédit. Par contre, mon père ne les aime pas.
   My mother finds that chip and pin cards are better than the older credit cards. However, my father doesn't like them.

4. **À n'importe quel prix = *whatever the price***
   Il faut que l'Irlande sorte de cette crise et ceci à n'importe quel prix.
   It is necessary that Ireland gets out of this crisis and this whatever the cost.

5. **Vouloir que + subjunctive = *to wish or want that...***
   Les professeurs veulent que les livres numériques soient disponibles pour les étudiants.
   Teachers want ebooks to be available for students.

6. **Ainsi que = *as well as***
   Les investisseurs internationaux cherchent une main-d'œuvre qualifiée ainsi que des subventions quand ils viennent pour créer des emplois.
   International investors look for a qualified work force as well as subsidies when they come to create jobs.

7. **Venir de = *to have just done something***
   Take the present tense of the verb venir + de + verb in the infinitive. eg: je viens de courir = I have just run.
   La commission européenne vient de verser les fonds européens.
   The European Commission has just paid out European funds.

8. **Il s'agit de = *it involves***
   Il s'agit d'un nouveau phenomène
   It involves a new phenomenon.

9. **Parvenir à + verb = *to manage to do something***
   Elle parvient à contrôler sa maison ainsi que son travail.
   She manages to control her house as well as her work.

10. **Pour y arriver = *in order to succeed***
    Pour bien réussir dans la vie, il faut tout faire pour y arriver.
    In order to succeed in life, it is necessary to do everything in order to succeed.

Dix expressions authentiques et ludiques

1. Ne pas lésiner sur les moyens = *to do everything in one's power to succeed*
2. Ça / il / elle me botte ! = *that or it suits me or pleases me*
3. Revoir sa copie = *to modify a plan in order to improve it*
4. Ne pas être dans son assiette = *to be out of sorts*
5. Ni quoi ni qu'est-ce = *nothing at all*
6. Être comme l'âne de Buridan = *to be indecisive, or to procrastinate*
7. Une tunique de Nessus = *a poisoned chalice*
8. Refiler la patate chaude = *to pass the buck*
9. River son clou (à quelqu'un) = *to cut someone to the quick, to injure someone emotionally*
10. Moucher quelqu'un = *to put someone back in their box*

CHAPITRE 6 — L'école

Aural Section

A — Les régles de l'école

Français	Anglais	How to pronounce
facile à vivre	*easygoing*	fah-seal ah viv
pendant	*during*	pon-don
exigé(e)	*demanded*	egg-zee-jay
réussir	*to succeed (regular verb)*	ray-ooh-sear

Remplissez les blancs

Il y a __des__ régles et il faut que tout le monde les respecte. Sinon c'est la __pagaille__ qui régne ! Dans mon école, le directeur/la directrice est __très__ facile à vivre, mais __il__ faut faire gaffe. Il ne faut pas dépasser les __limites__ de la tolérance. Les portables sont strictement __interdit__ et si vous avez votre __portable__ qui sonne pendant les __cours__ il est __confisqué__ pendant cinq jours. Il faut savoir que si on __n'obeit__ pas aux profs on peut être collé. Il y a __aussi__ pas mal de choses qui sont interdites. Une __tenue__ correcte est exigée. À part __tout__ ça, les professeurs nous __grondent__ moins et j'ai vraiment l'impression qu'ils __veulent__ qu'on fasse de notre mieux pour réussir. Il faut que l'on __puissent__ travailler en paix. On travaille pour ne pas __redoubler__, pour notre protection et pour passer une bonne __année__ scolaire. Sans règle, on s'évaderait de l'école. __Sans__ règles, on ferait tous les __fous__ et l'école ne servirait à rien. L'école est bien __structurée__ pour le bien-être __de__ tout le monde.

Bonne Chance!

B Le vandalisme dans les écoles et leurs environs

Français	Anglais	How to pronounce
une recrudescence	an abrupt rise	oone ray-cru-day-sonce
souvent	often	sue-von
les casiers	the lockers	lay caz-zee-ay
enfoncer (regular verb)	to break up	on-fon-say
gênant(e)	embarrassing, a nuisance	gen-non
aucun	no, not any	oh-kahn
des bandits	rogues	day bon-dee
la meilleure	the best (f)	la may-euhr

Answer the questions below.

1. Give one reason for the rise in acts of vandalism.
2. Give two examples of vandalism in schools.
3. What way could the money used to repair school furniture be used?
4. What happens to anyone caught vandalising school property?

C Le système de points

Français	Anglais	How to pronounce
une meilleure façon	a better way	oone may-yur fass-on
archaïque	archaic	ar-kye-eek
équitable	fair	ay-key-tabl
une licence	a degree	oone lee-sonce

Écoutez et répondez aux questions suivantes:

1. What does the author of the text find deplorable?
2. What solution does the author have to change the out-dated system?
3. What type of student does the points system favour according to this report?
4. What is the worst aspect of this system?
5. What type of system would the author prefer?
6. What is the author's hope for the future?

D Le harcèlement à l'école

Français	Anglais	How to pronounce
acceuillir	to welcome	ack-coy-ear
psychologue	psychologist	ip-see-co-log
un souffre-douleur	a scape goat	an soof-do-ler
honteux	ashamed	on-tuh
être conscient	to be conscious	et-re con-see-on
la réussite	success	la ray-oo-seat
le décrochage scolaire	dropping out of school	le day-cro-chaj skull-lair

1. Le calvaire de Paul a duré combien de temps ?
2. Pourquoi, d'après Paul, les victimes de la brimade ne veulent pas en parler aux parents ?
3. Selon les conseils de Julie, qu'est-ce qu'on peut faire si on est victime de la brimade ?
4. Rémplissez les blancs

    Patricia : J'étais _____ élève, j'avais _____ lunettes, mes camarades me _____ grosse et moche et j'étais nulle en _____ . Mes parents ont porté plainte me _____ un jour rentrer _____ des dessins dégradants sur les _____, mais sans résultat. Un jour, le directeur a dit aux élèves _____ de se calmer, mais ça a ____ une petite semaine. Après _____ années d'enfer, les _____ se sont calmés un ___ au lycée, j'ai encore des _____. J'ai fait une tentative de suicide en _____, alors que j'étais une élève brillante. Aujourd'hui je _____ d'un énorme problème de confiance en moi.

5. Selon Julie, quelles sont les conséquences d'être exposé à des comportements violents ?

    (a) _____
    (b) _____
    (c) _____

6. C'est un phénomène qui touche quelle pourcentage des élèves ?
7. Citez trois choses que vous pouvez faire pour sortir de la spirale du harcèlement.

    (a) _____
    (b) _____
    (c) _____

E — Est-ce que les diplômes sont nécessaires pour réussir dans la vie ?

Français	Anglais	How to pronounce
les qualifications	qualifications	lay kal-lee-fi-cass-yon
la concurrence	competition	la con-cure-ronce
être blindé	to be filled	et-re blan-day
réussir	to succeed	ray-ou-sear
précieux	precious, valuable	press-yuh

Write down how to say the following in French. Try them first without listening to the CD and then check to see how well you have done.

Anglais	Français
I would say	
it was normal	
required	
competition for jobs	
a university qualification	
a secure job	
to get on in life	
however	
formal training	
I can tell you	

F — Pour ou contre l'uniforme scolaire

Français	Anglais	How to pronounce
les établissements	establishments	lays ay-tab-bleese-mon
puisque	because	pweece-kuh
coûteux	expensive	coo-tuh
un pied d'égalité	an equal footing	an pea-ay day-galee-tay
gâcher	to spoil, to ruin	gash-shay

Écoutez puis répondez aux questions suivantes :

1. L'auteur nous donne plusieurs raisons pour porter l'uniforme scolaire. Nommez trois de ces raisons.

    (a) _____

    (b) _____

    (c) _____

2. À la fin de cet extrait, l'auteur nous donne trois raisons contre l'uniforme scolaire. Est-ce que vous pouvez nommer une de ces raisons ?

G Les écoles mixtes contre les écoles non-mixtes

Français	Anglais	How to pronounce
holistique	holistic	ol-iss-teek
pénible	annoying	pen-eeb-le
discours	speech	diss-coor
en avoir ras le bol	to be fed up	on-av-war ral-bol
envers	toward	on-vair

Listen to Paul and Rachel talk about their experience of school. Write down the order in which you hear the statements below from the text.

Statement	Number
behaviour in the school is more natural	
teachers demand that we work really hard this year	
the students are really united	
there are always those who tease others	
I am a bit shy toward girls	
results show that everyone can have the same success	
according to the statistics	
apart from the teachers and the classes	
it is good to be with friends	
I don't know if this type of education aids development	

H Leaving Cert 2012 Section III

Français	Anglais	How to pronounce
prochain	next	pro-shah
une matière	a subject	oone mat-tee-air
une filière	a course or subject	oone fil-lee-air
le trimestre	the term	le tree-mest-re

You will now hear a conversation between two teenagers, Karine and Joseph. The conversation will be played three times: first right through, then in four segments with pauses, and finally right through again.

1. Joseph says that the next class is:
    (a) Geography
    (b) Accounting
    (c) Chemistry
    (d) Engineering

Bonne Chance!

2. What do Karine's parents want her to do after leaving school?
3. Whom did Karine and her parents meet with?
    (a) Her guidance counsellor.
    (b) Her class teacher.
    (c) Her school principal.
    (d) Her maths teacher.
4. According to her parents, the career Karine would like is
    (a) dangerous to do
    (b) physically difficult
    (c) very badly paid
    (d) boring and tiring.

I Les faits divers

Français	Anglais	How to pronounce
toucher	to touch, to affect	too-shay
les mairies	the townhalls	lay may-ree
les collégiens	secondary school students (younger)	lay cull-lay-jian
les lycéens	secondary school students (older)	lay lee-see-en
systématique	systematic	sis-teh-ma-teek
attirer	to attract	ah-teer-ray

Article 1.
1. What has the supermarket chain Carrefour given to young victims of the recent tornado?

Article 2.
2. What have the members of the French parliament voted to ban?

Article 3.
3. When did research into bullying at school begin consistently?
4. The author mentions 6 countries. Name 3.

Oral Section – *Let's Get Talking*
Ten common questions on the subject of school

Français	Anglais	How to pronounce
Parlez-moi de votre école.	*Tell me about your school*	par-lay moi de votr ay-cul
Combien de profs y a-t-il dans votre école ?	*How many teachers are there in your school?*	com-bee-en de pruf ee-a-teel don votr ay-cul?
Que pensez vous de votre uniforme scolaire ?	*What do you think of your school uniform?*	kuh pon-say voo de votr oo-nee-form skull-air?
Quelles sont les matières que vous étudiez ?	*What subjects do you study?*	kell sohn lay mat-tee-air kuh vooz ay-tude-dee-ay?
Quelle est votre matière préférée ?	*What is your favourite subject?*	kel ay votr mat-tee-air pref-fer-ray?
Quelle est la matière que vous n'aimez pas et pourquoi ?	*What is the subject that you do not like and why?*	kel ay la mat-tee-air kuh voo nem-may pah ay poor-kwah?
Est-ce que vous trouvez que le réglement dans votre école est trop strict ?	*Do you find that the rules in your school are too strict?*	esse-kuh voo true-vay kuh le reg-le-mon don votr ay-cul ay tro streect?
Vous passez combien de temps à faire des devoirs tous les soirs ?	*How much time do you spend on your homework every evening?*	voo pas-say com-bee-en de ton a fair day dev-war too lay swar?
Que pensez-vous du système de points ?	*What do you think of the points system?*	kuh pon-say voo do sis-tem de pwan?
Si vous étiez le directeur / la directrice de votre école, quels changements mettriez-vous en place ?	*If you were the principal of your school, what changes would you put in place?*	see vooz et-tee-ay le deer-rec-ter / la deer-rec-treece de votr ay-cul kel change-mon met-ree-ay voo on plaace?

Dix questions et réponses possibles sur votre école

1. **Parlez-moi de votre école**
   Je suis dans une école pour garçons/filles uniquement/une école mixte. C'est un vieux bâtiment qui merite d'être retaper un peu. Cependant je sais que cela n'est pas une priorité pour notre gouvernement désargenté. Mon école s'est forgée une réputation aussi bien pour son excellence académique, que son allure sportive. Les professeurs exigent que nous travaillions d'arrache-pied cette année et c'est pénible d'entendre toujours le même discours.
   I am in an all boys/all girls school/mixed school. It is an old building that needs to be refurbished. However, I know that this is not a priority for our penniless government.

My school has forged a reputation as much for its academic excellence as its sporting prowess. The teachers insist that we work really hard this year, and its painful to have to always listen to the same speech.

2. **Combien de profs y a-t-il dans votre école ?**
   Il y a une trentaine de professeurs dans mon école.
   There are about 30 teachers in my school.

3. **Que pensez vous de votre uniforme scolaire ?**
   Pour moi, il y a de bonnes raisons pour le porter. D'abord puisque tout le monde est habillé pareil, personne ne se juge. Deuxièment, les uniformes sont bien moins coûteux que les vêtements à la mode que les élèves souhaitent généralement porter. Par contre, l'uniforme est souvent très moche. Il ne tient pas chaud en hiver et il est fort gênant en été.
   For me, there are good reasons to wear it. Firstly because everyone is dressed the same, nobody judges anyone. Secondly, uniforms are a lot less costly than fashionable clothes that students usually prefer to wear. However, the uniform is often very ugly. It doesn't keep you warm in the winter and it is very uncomfortable in the summer.

4. **Quelles sont les matières que vous étudiez ?**
   J'étudie sept matières dont l'irlandais, l'anglais et les maths sont obligatoires. En plus, je fais le français bien entendu et …
   I study seven subjects of which Irish, English and Maths are compulsory. On top of that I do French of course and… (add in your other three subjects.)

5. **Quelle est votre matière préférée ?**
   Je dois avouer que j'adore le français. Personnellement je pense que l'apprentissage d'une langue étrangère est une bonne façon de mettre tous les atouts dans son jeu. Cela vous permet de mieux comprendre les gens qui parlent cette langue, et on apprend beaucoup sur des cultures différentes. Sur le marché du travail, si vous avez une autre langue, c'est un sacré avantage. D'ailleurs le français est, avec l'anglais, la langue officielle de l'Europe.
   I must admit that I love French. Personally I think that learning a foreign language is a good way of leaving nothing to chance. It allows you to better understand the people who speak this language, and you learn a lot about different cultures. In the labour market, if you have another language it is a great advantage. As well as this, French is, along with English, the official language of Europe.

6. **Quelle est la matière que vous n'aimez pas et pourquoi ?**
   Je n'aime pas trop le/la/les *(add in subject)*. Je trouve que cette matière est fort difficile et je vois que je ne peux pas le/la/les capter. Le prof essaie de me faire comprendre mais pour moi, c'est une vraie épine dans le pied.
   I dont' really like (add in subject). I find that this subject is really difficult and I cannot grasp it. The teacher tries to make me understand but for me, it's a real thorn in my side.

7. **Est-ce que vous trouvez que le réglement dans votre école est trop strict ?**
   Oui et non. Il y a des régles et il faut que tout le monde les respecte. Sinon c'est la pagaille qui régne ! Les portables sont strictement interdits et si vous avez votre portable qui sonne pendant les cours, il est confisqué pendant cinq jours. Si on n'obéit

pas aux profs on peut être collé. Il y a aussi pas mal de choses qui sont interdites et une tenue correcte est exigée.
Yes and no. There are rules and everyone has to respect them. If not then it is chaos. Mobile phones are strictly forbidden and if you have your mobile phone which goes off in class, it is confiscated for five days. If we don't obey the teachers we can be given detention. There are also quite a lot of things which are forbidden and a proper uniform is expected.

8. **Vous passez combien de temps à faire des devoirs tous les soirs ?**
Bon cette année je passe environ quatre heures tous les soirs à faire mes devoirs et mes révisions. Je me donne de la peine cette année car je ne veux pas redoubler.
Right, this year I spend about four hours every evening doing my homework and my revision. I am going to the bother of it this year because I do not want to repeat.

9. **Que pensez-vous du système de points ?**
Je trouve que le système de points n'est pas équitable de tout ! D'abord il favorise ceux qui arrivent à retenir des choses par cœur. En plus, avec la chute économique, il y a plus de concurrence pour accéder à l'université. Le pire aspect de ce système est que souvent les points changent sans aucun avis.
I think that the points system isn't at all fair. Firstly it favours those who manage to learn things off by heart. On top of this, with the economic collapse, there is more competition to access university. The worst aspect of this system is that often the points change without warning.

10. **Si vous étiez le directeur / la directrice de votre école, quels changements mettriez-vous en place ?**
Bon. Je commencerais la journée à 10h pour donner aux élèves l'occasion de faire la grasse matinée. Je mettrais fin à la colle car c'est une idée ridicule. Il y aurait un complexe sportif dans l'école et finalement il y aurait une bonne cantine à l'école.
Well, I would start the day at 10 o'clock in order to give students the opportunity of having a lie-in. I would put an end to detention as it is a ridiculous idea. There would be a sports complex in the school and finally, there would be a good canteen.

Le Vocabulaire Essentiel

Français	Anglais	How to pronounce
le bon fonctionnement de	the proper working of	le bun funk-see-on-mon de
permettre	to allow	per-metr
mâcher du chewing gum	to chew chewing gum	mash-shay do shoe-ing gum
la colle	detention	la cull
l'expulsion	expelled	lex-pulse-yon
montrer l'exemple	to lead by example	mon-tray legs-zompl
les conséquences	consequences	lay con-say-conce

French	English	Pronunciation
une punition	*a punishment*	oone poo-niss-yon
injuste	*unfair*	an-joost
équitable	*fair*	ay-key-tab-le
une recrudescence	*a fresh outbreak of*	oone re-cru-de-sonce
une situation intolérable	*an intolerable situation*	oone sit-you-ass-yon an-tol-lair-rabl
jeter des affaires	*to throw things*	jet-tay days ah-fair
la loi	*the law*	la lwa
tagger	*to graffiti*	ta-gay
porter plainte	*to complain*	por-tay plant
vivre dans la peur	*to live in fear*	veev-re don la per
endommager	*to damage*	on-doh-mah-jay
saccager	*to wreck*	sack-ka-jay
être victime de	*to be a victim of*	et-re vic-teem de
l'éducation physique et sportive	*P.E.*	led-you-cass-yon fiz-zeek ay spor-teeve
viser	*to target*	vee-zay
la pratique	*the practice*	la pra-teek
le respect de soi-même et d'autrui.	*respect for oneself and for others*	le ress-pay de swa-mem ay doh-trwee
le soutien	*support*	le sue-tee-en
l'esprit d'équipe	*team spirit*	less-pree day-keep
se tenir comme des mollusques	*to act like wimps*	se ten-near com day mul-lusk
un atout pour réussir	*an asset for succeeding*	an ah-too poor ray-oo-sear
la réussite des élèves	*the success of pupils*	la ray-oo-seat days ay-lev
faire davantage de sport	*do more sport*	fair dav-von-taje duh spor
apprendre	*to learn*	ah-prond-re
embêtant	*annoying*	om-bet-ton
distraire	*to distract*	diss-trair
à la fin	*in the end*	a la fahn
indispensable	*vital, essential*	an-diss-pon-saabl
les effets négatifs	*negative effects*	lays ay-fay nega-teef
évidement	*of course*	ay-veed-ah-mon
une mentalité normale	*a normal mentality*	oone mon-tal-lee-tay nor-mal
doué(e)	*talented*	do-ay
provoquer	*to cause or to provoke*	pro-voh-kay
l'école est obligatoire	*school is compulsory*	lay-cul ay oh-blig-ga-twar
décider à l'avance	*to decide in advance*	de-sea-day ah la-vonce

Chapitre 6 L'école

une épreuve	*a test, an exam*	oone ay-preuv
obtenir	*to obtain*	ob-ten-neer
suivre des études	*to study*	sweev days ay-tude
mettre l'accent sur	*to emphasise*	met-lak-sawn soor
un cursus	*a course*	an cur-soose
le niveau supérieur	*honours level*	le nee-voh sue-per-ree-er
le niveau ordinaire	*ordinary level*	le nee-voh or-dee-nair
facultative	*optional*	fack-kul-ta-teeve
le souffre douleur	*the punching bag*	le soof-fr do-ler
subir des brimades	*to be bullied*	sue-beer day bree-mad
les grimaces	*making faces*	lay gree-mass
un geste grossier	*a vulgar gesture*	an jest grow-see-air
le pouvoir	*power*	le poo-vwar
persécuter	*to persecute*	per-seh-koo-tay
coupable	*guilty*	koo-pabl
la rivalité	*rivalry*	la ree-val-lee-tay
les plus faibles	*the weakest*	lay ploo faibl
infliger	*to inflict*	an-flee-jay
l'enseignant	*teacher*	lon-sen-yon
une vocation	*a vocation*	oone vo-cass-yon
l'envie d'apprendre	*the desire to learn*	lon-vee da-prondr
la gentillesse	*kindness*	la jon-tee-ess
s'en prendre à	*to pick on*	sawn-prondr ah
l'égalité	*equality*	lay-gal-lee-tay
consacrer	*to devote*	con-sack-ray
ausculter	*to examine (medically)*	ose-cule-tay
les activités pédagogiques	*educational activities*	lays ak-teev-vee-tay ped-da-go-jeek
toucher	*to affect, to touch, to earn*	too-shay
trouver sa voie	*to find one's way*	troov-ay sa vwah
parvenir	*to succeed*	par-ven-neer
la clef de la réussite	*the key to success*	la clay de la ray-oo-seat
le but ultime	*the ultimate goal*	le boo ul-teem
dans un premier temps	*firstly*	dons an prem-me-ay ton
heureux	*happy*	er-ruh
la réussite professionnelle	*professional success*	la ray-oo-seat pro-fess-see-oh-nal
un niveau de compétence	*a level of competence*	an nee-voh de com-peh-tonce

Bonne Chance!

les aptitudes scolaires	*scholarly apptitudes*	lays ap-tee-tude skull-lair
accéder	*to access*	ak-sed-day
la discrimination	*discrimination*	la diss-crim-min-nass-yon
c'est ridicule	*it is ridiculous*	say rid-dee-cule
la même manière	*the same way*	la mem man-nee-air
être restrictif	*to be restrictive*	et ress-treek-teef
porter	*to wear*	por-tay
l'écart	*the gap*	lay-car
c'est débile	*it is mad*	say de-beel
se faire niaiser	*to be taken for a ride*	se fair nee-ay-zay
vivre dans l'aisance	*to be well-off*	veevr don lez-zonce
un goût vestimentaire	*a taste in clothes*	an goo ves-tee-mon-tair
vivre en communauté	*to live with others*	veevr on com-moon-no-tay
partager	*to share*	par-ta-jay
supporter	*to put up, to tolerate*	sue-por-tay
mettre au point	*to finalise*	metr oh-pwan
l'angoisse	*anxiety, worry*	lon-gwass
un petit confort	*small comforts*	an pet-tee con-for
la froideur	*coldness*	la frwad-der
les régles	*rules*	lay regl
gérer	*to manage*	jair-ay
ruser	*to be crafty*	roo-zay

Dix constructions clés sur l'école

1. **À jour = *up to date***
   C'est important pour les étudiants de rester à jour avec les actualités.
   It is important for students to remain up to date with current affairs.

2. **Connu(e) pour = *known by + noun***
   Le directeur de l'école est connu pour son attitude d'impartialité.
   The principal of the school is known for his attitude of fairness.

3. **Ceux qui = *those who***
   Ceux qui travaillent bien à l'école sont toujours ceux qui arrivent dans la vie.
   Those who work well at school are always those who do well in life.

4. **En échange de = *in exchange for + verb in infinitive or noun***
   Je voudrais échanger mon emploi du temps chargé contre celui de ma sœur qui est à l'université.
   I would like to exchange my busy timetable for that of my sister, who is in university.

5. **Être en régression** = *to be in decline*
   Le niveau de harcèlement dans son école est en régression grâce aux mesures prises par la direction.
   The level of bullying in his school is in decline thanks to the measures taken by management.

6. **Être également en baisse** = *to also be in decline*
   Le nombre d'étudiants qui échouent au bac est également en baisse.
   The number of students who fail the leaving certificate is also in decline.

7. **C'est un moyen d'avoir** = *it's a way to have or of having*
   C'est un moyen d'avoir les meilleurs résultats.
   It is a way of having the best results.

8. **Contrairement à** = *contrary to*
   Contrairement à ce qu'on pense, la vie à l'école est souvent amusante.
   Contrary to what people think, life in school is often fun.

9. **Il ne peut rien y avoir de mieux que de + verb in the infinitive** = *there is nothing better than*
   Il ne peut rien y avoir de mieux que d'arriver en classe pour un examen et que le prof oublie de le donner.
   There is nothing betten than arriving in class for an exam and the teacher forgetting to give it.

10. **En ce moment** = *at the moment*
    Je ne peux pas sortir trop en ce moment car je dois me consacrer aux études.
    I cannot go out too much at the moment, because I have to devote myself to study.

Dix expressions authentiques et ludiques

1. Croquer le marmot = *to wait a long time moping*
2. Donner / recevoir une volée (de bois vert) = *to either give or receive a severe reprimand or criticism*
3. Enfiler des perles = *to waste one's time on stupidity*
4. Un cordon bleu = *an excellent chef*
5. Damer le pion = *to get the better of someone*
6. Travailler au noir / Faire du marché noir = *to work in the black market, illegally*
7. La cour des grands = *to enter into the big league*
8. Blanchir de l'argent = *to launder money*
9. Motus et bouche cousue = *to be completely discreet*
10. Avaler des poires d'angoisse = *to experience very tough situations or to be subjected to cruel treatment*

CHAPITRE 7 L'environnement

Aural Section

A Pourquoi payer l'eau

Français	Anglais	How to pronounce
le ciel	*the sky*	le see-ell
les usagers	*users*	lays oo-zaje-ay
financière	*financial*	fee-nonce-see-air

The following sentences and phrases are used in the text. Place them in the order in which you hear them.

Sentence	Number
The price of water treatment is rising.	
The service is free here.	
Everyone realises the importance of clean water.	
Less than 1% of all rain water is suitable for human consumption.	
In Ireland a lot of people are against the idea of paying for water.	
Users should pay a contribution.	
Everyone thinks that the water which falls from the sky is completely drinkable.	
whatever the cost	
in this country historical reasons explain the reticence of the people to pay	
in fact	
this is not always the case	
in order that	

B Les forêts tropicales

Français	Anglais	How to pronounce
la préservation	*preservation*	la prez-zer-vass-yon
les forêts	*forests*	lay for-ray
la déforestation	*deforestation*	la day-for-res-tass-yon
bénéfique	*beneficial*	ben-nay-feak
les nuages	*clouds*	lay new-aje

Listen to the extract on rain forests and fill in the blanks:

Il faut que nous _____ tous d'accord sur la préservation des forêts tropicales, car ceci est vraiment une _____ mondiale. Il nous _____ tous de réduire la déforestation des forêts tropicales. Selon une étude _____ en Suisse en 1989, planter et _____ des forêts tropicales pourraient ralentir le _____ climatique, alors que planter des forêts dans les hautes _____ pourrait contribuer au réchauffement. Ceci prouve que _____ les forêts tropicales sont fortement bénéfiques ____ ralentissement du réchauffement global car non seulement _____ absorbent le gaz carbonique mais elles _____ également les nuages qui aident à _____ la planète.

C L'énergie solaire

Français	Anglais	How to pronounce
l'énergie	*energy*	len-ner-jee
les besoins	*needs*	lay bez-wan
inépuisable	*inexhaustible*	in-ay-pweez-abl
efficace	*efficient*	ef-fee-cass
l'avenir	*the future*	lav-ven-neer

Listen to the extract and then answer the following questions.

1. Give three advantages of solar energy.
2. The sun sends the earth _____ times humanity's energy needs.
3. What is it still too early to see?
4. What is certain?

Bonne Chance !

D. Les déchets nucléaires

Français	Anglais	How to pronounce
les déchets	waste	lay deh-shay
les produits chimiques	chemical products	lay prod-wee shim-meek
le plomb	lead	le plon
les conséquences	consequences	lay con-say-konce
un incendie	a fire	an an-san-dee
nucléaire	nuclear	nook-lee-air

Listen to the CD and say whether the following statements are true or false.

Statement	True	False
1. If nuclear waste is well managed, there are no immediate risks.	✓	
2. The location of waste disposal units is crucial.	✓	✓
3. We cannot ignore the serious consequences of a fire in a storage area.	✓	
4. Solar energy cannot provide for a lot of our energy needs.	✓	✓
5. Solar energy will one day replace nuclear energy.	✓	

E. Le recyclage

Français	Anglais	How to pronounce
plusieurs	several	plooz-zee-er
quotidiennement	on a daily basis	co-tid-dee-en-mon
le chauffage	heating	le show-faaj
un arbre	a tree	an arb-r
un élément phare	a key element	an ele-mon far

Listen to the following young people talking and write down the order in which each of these is mentioned:

Item	Number
un élément phare	6
le recyclage	4
la production de nouvelles matières	2
chauffage	3
des arbres	5
l'essence	8
la pollution	1
le transport en commun	7
des produits recyclés	5 3.5

Chapitre 7 L'environnement

F Les inondations

Français	Anglais	How to pronounce
les inondations	*floods*	lays in-on-dass-yon
les catastrophes	*disasters*	lay cat-tass-trof
surveiller	*to watch / supervise*	sir-vay-ay
les dégâts	*damage*	lay day-ga
le reboisement	*reforestation*	le re-bwase-mon
malheureusement	*unfortunately*	mal-er-reuze-mon
surpeuplé	*over-populated*	sewer-pup-lay

Listen to the extract and then answer the following questions:

1. Il y avait combien de catastrophes naturelles en 2011 ?
2. Ces catastrophes naturelles ont tué combien de personnes ?
3. Qu'est-ce que l'auteur de cet article craint ?

G Leaving Cert 2003 Section 1

Français	Anglais	How to pronounce
la météo	*the weather forecast*	la met-tay-oh
la conscience	*awareness*	la conce-see-once
une coiffure	*a hair style*	oone cwof-fure
triste	*sad*	treest

Catherine Laborde, who presents the weather forecast on the French TV channel TF1, talks about her job. You will hear the material 3 times: first right through, then in three segments with pauses and finally right through again.

1. How did Catherine Laborde learn that TF1 had a vacancy for a weather forecast presenter?
2. (a) What does Catherine Laborde say to support her claim that the weather forecast is the most frequently watched programme on television?
   (b) What does she find surprising?
3. In what way, according to Catherine, does the job of a journalist/newsreader differ from that of a weather forecast presenter?

Bonne Chance !

H L'empreinte écologique

Français	Anglais	How to pronounce
l'empreinte	footprint	lamb-prant
la superficie	area, surface	la super-fiss-see
les hommes	men, mankind	lays um
éteindre	to turn off	ay-taandr
des appareils	devices, machinery	days ap-par-rye
le gaspillage	waste	le gas-pee-aje

Écoutez et puis remplissez les blancs.

Le terme _____ écologique est la _____ géographique nécessaire pour subvenir aux _____ d'une ville et absorber ____ déchets. Il faut être _____ à son usage personnelle. L'empreinte écologique _____ la pression exercée par les hommes _____ les ressources naturelles, _____ par la nature. Bien que l'idée ___ l'empreinte écologique soit quelque chose de scientifique, il nous incombe _____ d'être responsables et prudents. Chaque fois que nous quittons ___ pièce chez nous, c'est mieux _____ la lumière. Laisser des _____ allumés n'est jamais une bonne idée car ___ est du gaspillage. À l'école il faut fermer les _____ et _____ les lumières si la salle de classe est _____. Il faut bien vivre tout ___ respectant la nature. Elle est _____ puissante que nous et il faut qu'elle _____ appréciée par nous. C'est à nous _____ avant qu'il ___ soit trop tard ! Son empreinte est _____ de chacun.

I Les faits divers

Français	Anglais	How to pronounce
une difficulté	a difficulty	oone diffy-cul-tay
un ralentissement	a slow-down	an rah-lon-tiss-mon
le périphérique	the ring-road	le per-rif-fer-reek
la récolte	the harvest	la reh-cult
la pénurie	shortage	la pen-you-ree

Article 1.
1. What is the problem on the A25?

Article 2.
1. Give one reason why the grape harvest will be down by 40%.

Article 3.
1. When did this flooding happen?
2. How much is the damage estimated at?

Oral Section – *Let's Get Talking*
Ten common questions on the subject of the environment

Français	Anglais	How to pronounce
Est-ce que vous faites du recyclage à la maison ?	Do you do recycling at home?	esse-kuh voo fett do re-see-claj ah la may-zon?
Qu'est-ce qu'on peut faire pour réduire notre consommation d'énergie ?	What can we do to reduce our energy consumption?	kess-kon puh fair poor re-dweer notr con-so-mass-yon den-ner-jee?
Est-ce que vous pensez que les villes en Irlande sont propres ?	Do you think that the towns in Ireland are clean?	esse-kuh voo pon-say kuh lay veel on ear-lond sawn propr?
Que faites vous pour améliorer votre empreinte de carbone ?	What are you doing to improve your carbon footprint?	kuh fett voo poor ah-melly-oar-ay votr om-prant de car-bun?
Est-ce que vous prenez les transports en commun ?	Do you use public transport?	esse-kuh voo pren-nay lay tronz-por on co-man?
Comment faites-vous pour arriver à l'école ?	How do you get to school?	come-on fett voo poor ah-ree-vay ah lay-col?
Est-ce que vous pensez qu'il faut avoir des amendes pour jeter du papier et du chewing gum ?	Do you think that there should be fines for throwing papers and chewing gum?	esse-kuh voo pon-say kill fo av-war days ah-mond poor jet-tay doo pap-pea-ay ay doo shoe-ing gom?
Est-ce que vous pensez que nos plages en Irlande sont propres ?	Do you think that our beaches in Ireland are clean?	esse-kuh voo pon-say kuh no plaje on ear-lond sawn propr?

En Irlande nous n'avons pas trop de catastrophes naturelles. Quel est votre opinion ?	In Ireland we do not have many natural disasters. What is your opinion?	on ear-lond new nav-on pah tro de cat-tass-trough nat-tur-rel. kel ay votr oh-pin-yon?
Comment est-ce que nous pouvons aider les jeunes à mieux comprendre notre planète ?	How can we help young people to understand our planet better?	come-on esse kuh new poo-von ed-day lay jeun ah miu com-prond notr plan-net?

Dix questions et réponses possibles sur l'environnement

1. **Est-ce que vous faites du recyclage à la maison ?**
   Oui, nous avons une poubelle spéciale pour les déchets recyclables. Nous faisons le tri des déchets à la maison. Nous lavons les bouteilles et les bocaux. Mon père déchire les cartons et le papier et ma mère donne nos vieux vêtements aux associations caritatives. Je pense qu'il incombe à nous tous de recycler.
   Yes, we have a special bin for recyable waste. We sort out the rubbish at home. We wash bottles and food jars. My father rips up cardboard and paper and my mother gives our old clothes to charitable associations. I think that it is up to all of us to recycle.

2. **Qu'est-ce qu'on peut faire pour réduire notre consommation d'énergie ?**
   D'abord tout le monde peut aider dans cette démarche. Il faut simplement éteindre les lumières en sortant, utiliser les thermostats sur les radiateurs, penser à baisser le chauffage quand il fait moins froid, et éviter d'utiliser la climatisation dans les voitures.
   Firstly everyone can help in this process. We have to simply turn off lights when leaving, use thermostats on radiators, think about lowering the heating system when it's less cold, and avoid using the air conditioning in cars.

3. **Est-ce que vous pensez que les villes en Irlande sont propres ?**
   Je crois que la plupart de villes en Irlande sont assez propres, mais on peut toujours améliorer la propreté surtout dans les grandes villes. Il faut que tout le monde fasse de son mieux afin de garder nos villes propres.
   I believe that the majority of towns in Ireland are quite clean but we can always improve cleanliness, especially in the large cities. Everyone must do their best in order to keep our towns clean.

4. **Que faites-vous pour améliorer votre empreinte de carbone ?**
   Honnêtement, je ne fais pas trop attention à mon empreinte de carbone. Sans vraiment penser, je peux vous dire que je prends le vélo pour aller en classe ou bien je prends le bus. Je ne gaspille ni l'eau ni l'électricité. Je ne sais pas quoi d'autre.
   Honestly I don't pay much attention to my carbon footprint. Without really thinking I can tell you that I ride my bicycle to school or else I take the bus. I do not waste either water or electricity. I don't know what else.

5. **Est-ce que vous prenez les transports en commun ?**
Oui, je prends les transports en commun pour aller à l'école. C'est bien pratique sauf quand il y a une grève et alors là, c'est un cauchemar. Normalement je prends le bus avec mes potes et on rigole bien pendant le trajet.
Yes I use public transport to go to school. It is really handy except when there is a strike and then it's a nightmare. Usually I take the bus with my friends and we have a good laugh during the journey.

Non, je ne peux pas car j'habite trop loin de la ville et mon quartier n'est pas bien desservi. Je dois venir à l'école avec mon père tous les jours et il faut l'attendre après l'école. Parfois il est très en retard à cause des réunions au travail. J'aurais bien aimé habiter plus prés de mes amis mais mes parents ont construit notre maison en rase campagne.
No, I cannot because I live too far from the town and my area is not very well serviced. I must come to school with my father every day and I must wait for him after school. Sometimes he is very late because of meetings at work. I would have liked to live nearer to my friends, but my parents built our house in the middle of nowhere.

6. **Comment faites-vous pour arriver à l'école ?**
Comme j'habite à deux pas de l'école, je viens à pied / je prends le bus tous les matins / ma mère m'amène en voiture / je prends le Dart / je prends le Luas / je prends mon vélo, sauf quand il fait trop mauvais et à ce moment là, je prends des transports en commun.
As I live very near the school I come on foot/ I take the bus every morning/ my mother brings me in the car / I take the Dart/ I take the Luas / I take my bicycle except when the weather is too bad and then, I take public transport.

7. **Est-ce que vous pensez qu'il faut avoir des amendes pour jeter du papier et du chewing gum ?**
Oui sans l'ombre d'un doute il faut avoir des amendes pour ce genre de comportement. Les gens ne jetent pas les papiers ni le chewing gum dans leurs salons, donc il faut respecter les endroits publics aussi.
Yes, without the shadow of a doubt there must be fines for this type of behaviour. People don't throw paper or chewing gum in their sitting rooms so they should respect public areas also.

8. **Est-ce que vous pensez que nos plages en Irlande sont propres ?**
Il y a des plages qui sont très propres et il y a des plages qui ne sont pas trop propres. La plage que nous visitons tous les ans a le drapeau bleu et cela signifie qu'elle est bien propre. Il incombe à nous tous de garder nos plages aussi propre que possible. Si nous passons la journée à la plage, ma mère nous gronde si on met la pagaille.
There are beaches which are very clean and there are beaches which are not too clean. The beach that we visit every year has the blue flag and this shows that it is really clean. It is up to all of us to keep our beaches as clean as possible. If we spend the day at the beach, my mother tells us off if we make a mess.

9. **En Irlande nous n'avons pas trop de catastrophes naturelles. Quel est votre opinion ?**
   Oui c'est vrai qu'en Irlande nous avons de la chance d'avoir un climat plus ou moins tempéré. Ceci dit, il faut également constater que les inondations ces dernières années ont fait beaucoup de dégâts partout en Irlande. Je ne sais pas si cela est dû au mauvais temps ou si c'est le résultat des constructions mal finies.
   Yes, it is true that in Ireland we are lucky to have a temperate climate. Saying this, it must also be mentioned that the floods of the last few years did a lot of damage all over Ireland. I don't know if this is due to the bad weather or it is the result of badly-finished buildings.

10. **Comment est-ce que nous pouvons aider les jeunes à mieux comprendre notre planète ?**
    D'abord, je dirais que c'est très important pour les jeunes de comprendre notre planète. Je pense que l'éducation reste la clé. En plus, le gouvernement pourrait mener des campagnes à la télévision pour sensibiliser les jeunes. Notre avenir dépend de la planète et il faut que nous le sachions tous !
    Firstly, I would say that it is very important for young people to understand our planet. I think that education remains the key. On top of that, the government could launch campaigns on television to inform young people. Our future depends on the planet and we must all realise this!

Le Vocabulaire Essentiel

Français	Anglais	How to pronounce
les inondations	*floods*	lay in-on-dass-yon
des enjeux	*the stakes*	days on-juh
le niveau d'eau	*the level of water*	le nee-vo dough
la vitesse du courant	*the speed of the current*	la vee-tess do coor-ron
les risques de pollution	*the risk of pollution*	lay risk de pul-loose-yon
la crue	*the flood*	la krue
la prévention	*prevention*	la pray-vonce-yon
les sols	*soils*	lay sul
les pompiers	*firemen*	lay pomp-pee-ay
les équipes de sécurité civile	*civil defence teams*	lays ay-keep de say-cure-ree-tay sieve-veel
une cible	*a target*	oone seebl
inondable	*prone to flooding*	in-on-dabl
une barrière de fortune	*an improvised barrier*	oone bar-ree-air de for-tune
protéger provisoirement	*to protect provisionally*	pro-tege-jay pro-viz-war-mon
des dégâts matériels	*material damage*	day deh-ga ma-tear-ree-el
les pays pauvres	*poor countries*	lay pay-ee pauv

des accidents mortels	*fatal accidents*	day ak-see-don mor-tel
les catastrophes naturelles	*natural disasters*	lay cat-tass-trough nat-tur-rel
le cycle naturel des saisons	*the natural cycle of seasons*	le seekl nat-tur-rel day say-zon
une mousson	*a monsoon*	Oone moo-sohn
une réserve d'eau	*a water reserve*	oone ray-zerv dough
la saison séche	*the dry season*	la say-zon sech
une prise de conscience	*a realisation*	oone preez de conce-yonce
la fragilité	*the fragility*	la fra-jill-lee-tay
en amont	*upstream*	on ah-mon
l'entretien	*the maintenance*	lon-tre-chen
le reboisement	*the reforestation*	le re-bwase-mon
l'imperméabilisation urbaine	*urban sealing*	lam-per-meeb-bill-ass-yon ur-ben
le ruissellement	*the streaming down*	le rue-seal-mon
la lutte	*the fight*	la loot
une priorité mondiale	*a global priority*	oone pre-or-ree-tay mon-dee-al
les énergies renouvelables	*renewable energy*	lays en-nerge-ee reh-noov-vab
la tourbe	*peat*	la toorbe
le dioxyde de carbone	*carbon dioxide*	le dee-ox-seed de car-bon
les émissions de carbone	*carbon emissions*	lays ay-miss-yon de car-bon
le réchauffement planétaire	*planetary warming*	le reh-shauf-mon plan-neh-tair
les pays en voie de développement	*developing countries*	lay pay-ee on voye de dev-vel-up-mon
les incendies	*fires*	lays an-son-dee
la terre	*the earth*	la tair
le ralentissement	*the slowing down*	le rah-lon-tiss-mon
l'effet de serre	*greenhouse effect*	lef-fay de sair
les combustibles fossiles	*fossil fuels*	lay com-bus-teeb foss-seal
le méthane	*methane*	le meh-tane
la couche d'ozone	*the ozone layer*	la cooch doh-zone
à ce jour	*up to today*	ah se-jure
augmenter en flèche	*to go up really quickly*	og-mon-tay on flesh
la croissance	*growth*	la cwass-sonce
le pétrole	*oil*	le pet-rull
le charbon	*coal*	le shar-bon
le gaz naturel	*natural gas*	le gaze nat-ture-el

French	English	Pronunciation
illimitée	*limitless*	ee-lim-ee-tay
disponible	*available*	diss-pon-neeb
l'énergie solaire	*solar energy*	len-erg-ee soh-lair
les puissances occidentales	*western powers*	lay pwee-sonce ox-see-don-tal
l'avenir énergétique	*energy future*	lav-ven-neer en-er-jet-teek
les panneaux solaires	*solar panels*	lay pan-noh soh-lair
une énergie inépuisable	*an inexhaustible energy*	oone en-er-jee in-ay-pweez-ab
la chaleur	*heat*	la sha-lur
l'entretien	*the maintenance*	lon-tret-tian
une dépense	*an expense*	oone day-ponce
une ressource énergétique	*an energy resource*	oone reh-soorce en-er-jet-teek
atteindre	*to reach, to achieve*	ah-taand
fournir	*to provide*	foor-neer
l'occident	*the west*	lox-see-don
une meilleur solution	*a better solution*	oone may-er soh-luce-yon
inciter	*to incite*	an-see-tay
les objets usagés	*used objects*	lays ob-jay oo-zah-jay
le tri	*the sorting*	le tree
la fabrication	*the manufacture*	la fah-bree-cass-yon
les papiers	*paper*	lay pap-pee-ay
le carton	*cardboard*	le car-ton
l'industrialisation	*industrialisation*	lan-dus-tree-al-ease-zass-yon
la gestion	*the management*	la jest-yon
un produit recyclable	*a recyclable product*	an pro-dwee re-seek-lab
le ramassage	*the collection*	le ram-mass-aje
mettre en place	*to put in place*	met-on-plass
le stockage	*the storage*	le stoc-caje
la qualité de l'air	*air quality*	la cal-lee-tay de lair
les changements climatiques	*climate change*	lay change-mon clee-ma-teek
le protocole de Kyoto	*the Kyoto protocol*	le proto-col de key-oh-toe
incinéré	*incinerated*	an-sin-ner-ray
un centre de tri	*a sorting centre*	an sont de tree
des outils	*tools*	days oo-tee
le papier d'emballage	*packaging*	le pap-pee-ay dom-bal-laje
les boîtes de conserve	*food tins*	lay bwat de con-serve
les pneus	*tyres*	lay peh-nuh

les déchets synthétiques	synthetic waste	lay deh-shay san-teh-teek
l'empreinte	the footprint	lom-prant
mesurer	to measure	mez-zoo-ray
absorber	to absorb	ab-zor-bay
compte tenu	considering	cont ten-nu
la durabilité	durability	la duar-rah-bil-lee-tay
une question scientifique	a scientific question	oone kest-yon see-on-tif-feek
surexploiter	over exploit	sewer-ex-ploit-tay
la comptabilité	accountability	la comp-ta-bil-lee-tay
l'ensemble de	the totality of	lon-somb de
la soutenabilité	sustainability	la sue-ten-ah-bil-lee-tay
l'entité	the entity	lon-tee-tjeh
réversible	reversable	re-ver-seeb
les surfaces agricoles	agricultural area	lay soor-fass ag-ree-cul
le marché de la construction	the construction market	le mar-shay de la con-strooks-yon
la crise du logement	the accommodation crisis	la creeze do loje-mon
s'effondrer	to crumble	say-fond-ray
un repli	a withdrawal, a falling back	an reh-plee
un rabotage	a planing down	an rab-bo-taje
un chantier	a building site	an shon-tee-ay
l'économie	the economy	lay-con-no-mee
un permis de construire	planning permission	an per-mee de conce-tweer

Dix consructions et réponses clés sur l'environnement

1. **Il est également fort probable que** = *it is highly likely that*
   Il est également fort probable que les dégâts auraient pu être évités.
   It is highly likely that the damage could have been avoided.

2. **Être défini par** = *to be defined by*
   Un ouragan est défini par des pluies torrentielles et des vents très forts.
   A hurricane is defined by torrential rain and very heavy winds.

3. **Force agissante** = *the driving force*
   Quelle est la force agissante derrière le réchauffement climatique ?
   What is the driving force behind global warming?

4. **Rendre + noun + adjective** = *to make something something*
   La technologie rend la vie plus facile.
   Technology makes life easier.

   La protection des espèces rend leur survie plus certaine.
   The protection of species makes their survival more certain.

5. **Sans que nous le sachions** = *without us knowing it* (can be used in a variety of topics for the LC)
   Il peut avoir d'autres catastrophes naturelles dans les endroits le plus écartés du monde sans que nous le sachions.
   There may be more natural disasters in the most remote areas of the world without us knowing it.

6. **On peut avoir** = *we can have*
   On peut avoir des campagnes pour lutter contre la pollution.
   We can have campaigns to fight against pollution.

7. **N'importe quelle question** = *whatever question*
   Il peut répondre à n'importe quelle question. C'est un politicien sans égal.
   He can answer whatever question. He is a politician without parallel.

8. **Il semble que** = *it seems that*
   Il semble que notre gouvernement ne fait pas assez pour aider les marginaux de notre societé.
   It seems that the government is not doing enough to help those who live on the margins of our society.

9. **Une chose est certaine** = *one thing is certain*
   Malgré les initiatives prises par le gouvernement, une chose est certaine, on ne peut pas ignorer ce problème.
   Despite initiatives taken by the government, one thing is certain, we cannot ignore this problem.

10. **Il ne faut pas oublier que** = *we must not forget that*
    Il ne faut oublier que les inondations qui ont ravagé l'île Maurice ont fait une dizaine de morts.
    We must not forget that the floods that ravaged Mauritius left a dozen people dead.

Dix expressions authentiques et ludiques

1. Il n'est pas à prendre avec des pincettes = *he is in very bad form*
2. Faire main basse sur… = *to take or to steal*
3. En bonne et due forme = *within the rules*
4. On ne peut à la fois être juge et partie = *we cannot be both judge and jury*
5. Outre mesure = *unduly or excessively*
6. L'exception (qui) confirme la règle = *the exception confirms the rule*
7. Dare-dare = *immediately*
8. Une madeleine de Proust = *a memory trigger*
9. Donner le coup de collier / (re)prendre le collier = *to put one's back into it*
10. La poudre de perlimpinpin = *snake oil, a remedy that people claim to be miraculous but which does not work at all*

CHAPITRE 8 — La santé

Aural Section

A. La nourriture de mauvaise qualité

Français	Anglais	How to pronounce
la nourriture	food	la noor-ree-tur
du poids	weight	do-pwah
empêcher	to prevent	om-pey-shay
les publicités	ads	lay pub-li-sea-tay
le grignotage	snacking	le grin-nyo-tage
sinon	if not	see-noh

Remplissez les blancs.

On ne peut pas _____ que la nourriture de mauvaise qualité et sa surconsommation est un facteur énorme de _____. Lorsque les enfants consomment plus de calories qu'ils n'en _____, ils prennent eux aussi du poids. La restauration _____ est partout; le pizza, le poulet frites, les hamburgers. Pourtant, ce n'est pas possible d'empêcher les _____ de les manger quand ils sont en _____ ou avec leurs copains, alors que les parents essayent de leur montrer un _____ alimentation sain. C'est tout à fait simple de rendre responsable les publicités de bonbons et de prêt-à-mangers. Personnellement, je suis de _____ que si les parents achètent la nourriture pour leurs enfants, c'est eux qui _____ être responsable de leurs régimes alimentaires. Les jeunes adorent manger les _____ et le fast food. C'est trop facile de préparer un _____ que de préparer un bon repas traditionel et ____ dit, le grignotage n'est pas de tout _____. Il faut que les jeunes mangent à leur _____, mais il faut que cela soit varié et équilibré. Sinon, ce type de régime peut _____ les problèmes de santé plus tard dans la vie.

B   Des risques de santé pour les jeunes

Français	Anglais	How to pronounce
un problème croissant	*a growing problem*	an prob-lem crwass-aun
souvent	*often*	sue-von
surtout	*especially*	soor-too
coincé	*cornered or stuck*	quawn-say
trouver un moyen	*to find a way*	trou-vay ann moy-an
des sentiments	*feelings*	day saun-tee-mau
un fléau	*a scourge*	an flay-oh
un boulot	*a job (familiar)*	an boo-lo
financièrement	*financially*	fee-non-see-air-mon
évitable	*avoidable*	ay-vee-tabl
une aiguille	*a needle*	oone ay-gwee

Listen to the following four people talk about what they consider to be the major health risks for young people today, then fill in the grid below.

Name	Health Risk	One point about the risk	Result of this risk
Claudine			
Thomas			
Marie-France			
Jean-Michel			

C   Le cancer

Français	Anglais	How to pronounce
l'organisme	*the body*	lor-gan-neez-meh
maligne	*malignant*	mah-lean
envahir	*to invade*	on-vye-ear
essaimer	*to spread*	ess-sem-may
pénible	*troublesome*	pen-neebl
l'espérance	*hope*	less-pear-ronce
le dépistage	*the detection*	le day-piss-taje
auparavant	*before, formerly*	oh-para-von
renoncer	*to give up*	re-non-say

Écoutez puis répondez aux questions suivantes:

1. Expliquez le terme général de cancer.
2. Donnez un trait caractéristique du cancer.
3. Qu'est-ce qu'on peut faire pour minimiser le risque de développer le cancer ?

D L'obésité

Français	Anglais	How to pronounce
le surpoids	*excess weight*	le sur-pwah
cette maladie	*this disease*	set mal-lah-dee
sédentarité	*sedentary lifestyle*	suh-den-tar-ree-tay
l'hypertension artérielle	*high blood pressure*	leap-per-tonce-yon ar-ter-ree-el
les pays occidentaux	*western countries*	lay pay-ee ox-sea-don-toe
nuire	*to damage or endanger*	nweer
en vieillissant	*ageing*	on vee-ay-ee-son
un fardeau	*a burden*	an far-doe

Answer the questions below.

1. Which sentence was mentioned in the passage?
    (a) Obesity concerns over 1.7 million people world-wide
    (b) Obesity concerns just under 1.7 million people world-wide
2. Which sentence was mentioned in the passage?
    (a) The reasons behind this disease are very well understood
    (b) The reasons behind this disease are quite well understood
3. The article mentions 5 consequences of obesity. Name 2 of these.
4. Explain obesity at its most basic level.
5. What is the World Health Organisation in French?
    O--------- M-------de la S----.
6. What have health professionals predicted?
7. How will obesity eventually lead to depression?

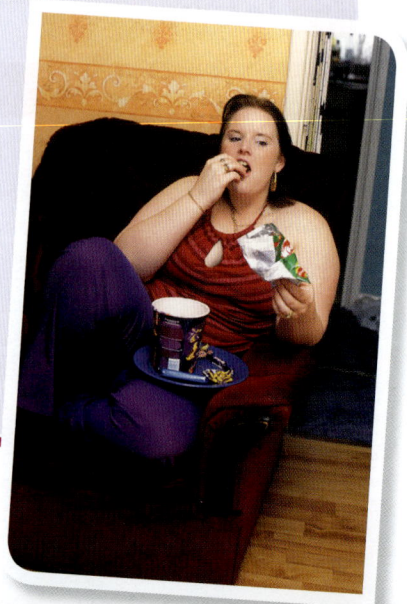

E L'anorexie

Français	Anglais	How to pronounce
une préoccupation	a concern or worry	oone prey-ock-queue-pass-yon
les mécanismes	the triggers	lay mek-can-nees-meh
incriminer	to blame	ann-crim-mee-nay
maigreur	thinness	meg-reur
éveiller	to arouse (suspicion)	ay-vay-ay
aveuglé par	blinded by	ah-vug-glay par

Listen and number the following statements in the order in which you hear them.

Statement	Number
imitation between teenagers is often blamed	
the causes are unknown	
it is often the case	
those who suffer from this awful disease	
less serious	
less serious eating disorders	
one out of ten teenagers	
the school results	
we often find a psychological disturbance in relation to body image	
it remains difficult	
the triggers are probably complex	
anorexia brings about drastic nutritional restrictions	

F Les organismes génétiquement modifiés

Français	Anglais	How to pronounce
les organismes génétiquement modifiés	genetically modified organisms	lays or-gan-nees-meh jen-neh-teak-mon mod-diff-fee-ay
controversé	controversial	con-trow-ver-say
en vigueur	in force or applicable	on vee-gur
les renseignements	information or details	lay ron-sen-yeh-mon
les équilibres	the equilibrium or balance	lays ay-kil-leebr
la faim	hunger	la fahn
la sécheresse	drought	la sesh-ress
un moratoire	moratorium	ann mora-twaar

Listen then answer the following questions:

1. The presence of Genetically Modified Organisms in food and in the environment:
   (a) Raises moral questions
   (b) Raises some questions
   (c) Raises many questions

2. Complete the following sentence in English.
   The subject of GMOs is more or less _____ according to the _____ the values of its _____ and the _____ in place. Eventhough different _____ of information exist about GMOs, _____ opinions about them can leave one _____.

3. Who profits from Genetically Modified Organisms?

4. Complete the following sentence in English.
   It is they that say that GMOs will put an end to _____ throughout the _____, but according to studies, _____ of genetically modified _____ do not have a _____ superior to traditional cereals. They do not _____ drought either.

5. How many countries have established a national moratorium in order to forbid the growing of GMOs on their soil?

6. How has France justified its decision?

G Leaving Cert 2001 Section II

Français	Anglais	How to pronounce
renoncer à	to give up	ruh-non-say
des effets	effects	days eff-fay
le poids	weight	le pwaw
jamais	never	jah-may
être fier	to be proud	et-re fee-air

This material will be played three times: first right through, then in four segments, with pauses and finally, right through again.

1. Name one of the emotional states which led Christine to smoke.

2. Christine had been smoking for
   (a) 5 years
   (b) 13 years
   (c) 15 years
   (d) 50 years

Bonne Chance!

3. Since she gave up smoking, Christine has:
   (a) Put on weight
   (b) Lost weight
   (c) Suffered headaches
   (d) Saved money

4. Why is she particularly proud to have given up smoking?

H Les faits divers

Français	Anglais	How to pronounce
un trafiquant	*a drug-dealer*	an traf-fee-kon
l'héroïne	*heroin*	ler-ro-een
surtout	*especially*	soor-too

Article 1.
1. How much heroin did the police find?

Aricle 2.
1. Who will be on strike tomorrow?
2. What is their principal demand?

Article 3.
1. What does this piece of research show?

Oral Section – *Let's Get Talking*
Ten common questions about the subject of health

Français	Anglais	How to pronounce
Que feriez vous si vous étiez ministre de la santé pour améliorer notre système de santé ?	*What would you do to improve our health system if you were minister for health?*	kuh fair-ree-ay voo see vooz et-tee-ay min-niece-tr de la sawn-tay poor ah-melly-oar-ay notr sis-tem de sawn-tay?
Est-ce que vous mangez équilibré ?	*Do you eat a balanced diet?*	esse-kuh voo mon-jay ay-keel-leeb-ray?
À votre avis, pourquoi il y a tant d'enfants obèses ?	*In your opinion, why are there so many obese children?*	ah votr ah-vee poor-kwah il ee ah ton don-fon oh-bez?
Que faites-vous pour rester en bonne santé ?	*What do you do to stay healthy?*	kuh fett voo poor res-tay on bun sawn-tay?
Que doivent faire les parents afin d'empêcher l'obésité chez leurs enfants ?	*What must parents do to prevent obesity in their children?*	kuh dwave fair lay par-ron ah-fan dom-pech-shay lo-bez-zee-tay shay leurz on-fon?
Est-ce que vous buvez de l'alcool ?	*Do you drink alcohol?*	esse-kuh voo boo-vay de lal-col
Est-ce que vous pensez que les jeunes en Irlande boivent trop d'alcool ?	*Do you think that young people in Ireland drink too much alcohol?*	esse-kuh voo pon-say kuh lay jeun on ear-lond bwoive tro dal-cul
Qu'est-ce que vous mangez à midi ?	*What do you eat at lunch time?*	kess-kuh voo mon-jay ah mid-dee?
Est-ce que vous donnez un coup de main pour préparer des repas à la maison ?	*Do you give a hand to prepare meals at home?*	esse-kuh voo don-nay an coo de man poor pre-par-ray day re-pah a la may-zon?
Quel est votre plat favori ?	*What is your favourite food?*	kel ay votr pla fa-vor-ree?

Dix questions et réponses possibles sur la santé

1. **Que feriez-vous si vous étiez ministre de la santé pour améliorer notre système de santé ?**
   Si j'étais ministre de la santé j'exigerais que les hôpitaux soient responsables. Je mettrais fin aux listes d'attentes et je ferais des visites imprévues dans les lieux pour voir si les choses fonctionnent bien comme il faut.
   If I was the minister for health, I would demand that hospitals be held accountable. I would put an end to waiting lists and I would make unexpected visits to places to see if things were working like they should be.

2. **Est-ce que vous mangez équilibré ?**
   Oui, normalement je mange bien. J'aime bien grignoter de temps en temps et cette année j'ai toujours des bonbons à portée de main. Il n'y a aucun doute qu'il y a beaucoup de jeunes de nos jours qui sont stressés par leur poids. Je mange des légumes et des fruits et je pense que si son régime est varié et sain on n'a pas besoin de maigrir.
   Yes, usually I eat well. I love snacking from time to time and this year, I always have sweets within arm's reach. There is no doubt that there are a lot of young people nowadays who are stressed by their weight. I eat vegetables and fruit and I think that if one's diet is varied and healthy, one does not need to slim down.

3. **À votre avis, pourquoi il y a tant d'enfants obèses ?**
   Il y a tant d'obésité chez les enfants car les parents sont trop occupés pour préparer des repas sains à la maison. Ils achètent des repas surgelés et ils les mettent dans le micro-onde au lieu de préparer des repas à partir de zéro. En plus, les enfants ne sortent pas beaucoup et ils restent scotchés devant la télévision.
   There is so much obesity among children because parents are too busy to prepare healthy meals at home. They buy frozen meals and put them in the microwave instead of making meals from scratch. On top of this, children do not go out a lot and they stay glued to the television.

4. **Que faites-vous pour rester en bonne santé ?**
   D'abord je fais attention à ce que je mange. Je fais du sport et je fais des promenades.
   Firstly I am careful about what I eat. I do sport and I go for walks.

5. **Que doivent faire les parents afin d'empêcher l'obésité chez leurs enfants ?**
   Il faut que les parents montrent l'exemple à leurs enfants. Il faut que les enfants voient que leurs parents mangent bien comme il faut et ils feront pareil. Les enfants ne sont pas fautifs dans l'affaire. C'est aux parents de faire en sorte que les enfants mangent des légumes et des fruits et qu'ils évitent les sucreries quand c'est possible.
   Parents must set an example to their children. Children must see their parents eating properly and they will do the same. Children are not at fault here. It is up to the parents to do what is necessary in order that children eat vegetables and fruit and that they avoid sweet things when possible.

6. **Est-ce que vous buvez de l'alcool ?**
   Oui, je bois de l'alcool de temps en temps, mais cela n'est pas une habitude. Je ne bois pas en cachette. Je bois surtout pendant les fêtes de famille ou si je sors avec la bande. Je ne bois que deux verres à peu près car je ne veux pas avoir la gueule de bois le lendemain.
   Yes, I drink alcohol from time to time, but it is not a habit. I don't drink in secret. I drink especially during family gatherings or if I go out with the gang. I only drink about two drinks because I do not want to have a hangover the following day.

   Non, je ne bois pas de tout. Je trouve que c'est moche de voir quelqu'un ivre donc, je ne veux jamais être dans un état pareil.
   No, I do not drink at all. I think that it is ugly to see someone drunk so I don't ever want to be in a similar state.

7. **Est-ce que vous pensez que les jeunes en Irlande boivent trop d'alcool ?**
Partout dans le monde, les Irlandais ont une réputation pour leur consommation d'alcool. Je pense que cette réputation est bien méritée. Après la fermeture des bars en Irlande, on peut observer tous les fous de la ville. Il y a toujours des jeunes qui boivent trop et c'est dégoutant de voir un tel comportement. C'est vraiment moche.
Everywhere in the world, the Irish have a reputation for their alcohol consumption. I think that this reputation is well deserved. After the closing of pubs in Ireland, you can see all the mad people from the town. There are always young people who drink too much and it is disgusting to see such behaviour. It is really ugly.

8. **Qu'est-ce que vous mangez à midi ?**
En France, les jeunes mangent un repas à la cantine avec une entrée, un plat principal et un dessert. En Irlande nous mangeons quelque chose vite fait comme un sandwich ou un peu de potage. Généralement j'amène un sandwich, des fruits, un yaourt et une boisson.
In France, young people eat a meal at the canteen with a starter, a main course and a dessert. In Ireland, we eat something quick like a sandwich or some soup. Generally I bring a sandwich, some fruit, a yogurt and a drink.

9. **Est-ce que vous donnez un coup de main pour préparer des repas à la maison ?**
Parfois je donne un coup de main à la maison pour préparer des repas, mais c'est ma mère qui fait tout. Elle est femme au foyer et c'est super de rentrer à la maison et de bien manger.
Sometimes I give a hand at home to prepare meals, but it is my mother who does everything. She is a stay-at-home mother and it is super to return home and eat well.

Oui, je donne un coup de main presque tous les soirs car mes parents travaillent et je rentre en premier. J'épluche les pommes de terre et je mets la viande au four. Ça dépend du jour mais en général, c'est moi qui fais tout.
Yes I give a hand almost every evening because my parents work and I return home first. I peel the potatoes and put the meat into the oven. It depends on the day, but in general, it is me who does everything.

10. **Quel est votre plat favori ?**
J'adore les pâtes. Je pourrais en manger tous les jours !
I love pasta. I could eat it every day!

Le Vocabulaire Essentiel

Français	Anglais	How to pronounce
le grignotage	snacking	le grin-no-taj
les sucreries	sweets, cakes	lay sook-reh-ree
un goûter	a snack (afternoon tea)	an goo-tay
un en-cas	a snack	an on-ka
une quantité suffisante	a sufficient quantity	oone qwan-tee-tay sue-fee-zont
une sensation de satiété	a feeling of being satisfied	oone sawn-sass-yon de sass-see-ay-te-tay
diététicienne	dietician	dee-ay-te-tiss-see-en
diversifié	varied	dee-ver-sif-fee-ay
le comportement à table	table manners	le com-port-mon ah tabl
une alimentation saine	healthy food	oone ali-mon-tass-yon sen
souffrir	to suffer	soof-rear
les ingestions excessives	excessive eating	lays an-jest-yon ek-sess-seev
provocation du vomissement	to cause vomiting	pro-vo-cass-yon du vom-mis-mon
l'utilisation inappropriée	in appropriate usage	loo-til-ease-zass-yon in-ap-pro-pree-ay
une combinaison de facteurs	a combination of factors	oone com-bin-naze-yon de fac-ter
indomptable	unmanageable	an-dompt-tabl
un caractère	a personality trait	an car-ak-tair
maîtriser	to master	may-tree-zay
nuire à la santé	to damage one's health	nweer ah la sawn-tay
concerner	to concern or affect	con-sir-nay
un pouvoir invasif	an invasive power	an poo-vwar an-va-seef
les cellules du corps	the cells of the body	lay sell-ule do cor
les facteurs de risques	risk factors	lay fac-ter de reesk
le dépistage	the detection	le de-peess-taj
menacer	to threaten	men-nass-say
l'irradiation	radiation	lear-rad-dee-ass-yon
cancérigène	carcinogenic	con-sair-ee-jen
les facteurs hormonaux	hormonal factors	lay fac-ter or-mon-oh
une tumeur maligne	a malignant tumour	oone too-mer mal-lean
un comportement anormal	abnormal behaviour	an com-por-tay-mon ah-nor-mal

le syndrome de l'immunodéficience acquise (SIDA)	auto-immune deficiency syndrome (AIDS)	le san-drom de lim-muno-deffy-see-ance ah-keys (see-dah)
une pandémie	a pandemic	oone pan-dem-mee
la guérison	the cure	la gair-ree-zon
la prolifération	the proliferation	la pro-lif-fer-rass-yon
un traitement efficace	an effective treatment	an tret-mon effy-cass
la lutte	the fight or battle	la loot
un sidéen	an aids sufferer	an sid-dee-en
éradiquer	to eradicate	ay-rad-dee-kay
les hémophiles	haemophiliacs	lays ay-mo-feel
le mode de transmission	way of transmission	le mud de tronz-miss-yon
un événement stressant	a stressful event	an ay-ven-mon stress-on
une réaction en chaîne	a chain reaction	oone ray-axe-yon on shen
le cerveau	the brain	le sir-voh
la fuite	flee or escape	la fweet
l'attaque	the attack	la-tak
l'immobilisation	frozen (with fear for example)	lee-mo-bil-ease-ass-yon
apaiser	to ease	ah-pez-zay
un traumatisme	a trauma	an traw-ma-tease-meh
la définition médicale	the medical definition	la def-fin-iss-yon med-dee-cal
la perception	the perception	la per-seps-yon
un trouble mental	a mental problem	an troobl mon-tal
la perte d'espoir	loss of hope	la pert dess-pwar
l'envie	interest in or desire for something	lon-vee
la fatigue	tiredness	la fa-teege
la tristesse	sadness	la tris-tess
les idées noires	black thoughts	lays ee-day nwar
l'angoisse	worry	lon-gwass
l'Organisation Mondiale de la Santé.	World Health Organisation	lorg-in-nass-yon mon-dee-al de la sawn-tay
dépressif	depressing	de-press-seef
la dépression clinique	clinical depression	la deh-press-yon clin-neek
l'obésité	obesity	lo-bez-zee-tay
la vie sédentaire	sedentary life	la vee sed-don-tair
des facteurs héréditaires	hereditary factors	day fac-ter air-red-dee-tair
manger en cachette	to eat in secret	mon-jay on cash-shet
la honte	shame	la ont
le comportement	behaviour	le com-port-mon

French	English	Pronunciation
d'ores et déjà	here and now	doorz ay de-jah
la corpulence	overweight	la cor-pu-lawnse
vraisemblablement	evidently	vray-som-bla-ble-mon
le surpoids	overweight	le soor-pwah
une perturbation psychologique	a psychological disturbance	oone per-ter-bass-yon psee-col-lo-jeek
la mode	fashion	la mud
les adolescents	teenagers	lays ado-less-son
incriminer quelqu'un	to incriminate or blame someone	an-crim-mee-nay kel-kan
la perte d'appétit	the loss of appetite	la pert dap-pet-tee
estime en soi	self esteem	es-teem on swa
la concurrence	competition	la con-cure-ronce
la guérisson	the cure	la gair-ree-son
l'image du corps	body image	lee-maj do cor
perdre des kilos	to lose a lot of weight	perdr day kee-lo
les organismes génétiquement modifiés	genetically modified organisms	lays or-gan-nees-meh jen-ne-teek-mon mod-diff-fee-ay
fiable	reliable	fee-abl
les opinions divergentes	differing opinion	lays oh-pin-yon dee-ver-jont
l'agriculture intensive	intensive farming	lag-ree-cul-ture an-ton-seeve
les mises à jour	updates	lay meez ah jure
une agriculture écologique	ecological agriculture	oone ag-ree-cul-ture ay-col-oh-jeek
des aliments sains	healthy food	days ali-mon sen
utilisation massive de pesticides	widespread use of pesticides	oo-til-ease-zass-yon mah-seeve de pes-ti-seed
des études scientifiques	scientific studies	days ay-tude see-on-tee-feek
les données	data	lay don-nay
boire à jeun	to drink on an empty stomach	bwar ah jon
boire coup sur coup	to knock back drink	bwar coo sur coo
avoir de l'embonpoint	to be carrying a few extra pounds	av-war de lom-bon pwan
se donner le tournis	to make oneself dizzy	se don-nay le tur-nee
le réseau sanguin	the bloodstream	le ray-zo sawn-gueen
gâcher une soirée	to ruin an evening	gash-shay oone swar-ray
se retrouver dans un état piteux	to find oneself in a pitiful state	se re-troov-ay dons an ay-ta pit-yuh
le foie	the liver	le fwa
une consommation raisonnable	a reasonable consumption	oone con-so-mass-yon res-zon-abl
une tête de cloche	a hangover	oone tet de clush

Chapitre 8 La santé

Dix constuctions clés sur la santé

1. **On parle souvent de** = *we often speak about*
   On parle souvent d'une alimentation saine.
   We often speak about healthy food.

2. **Quel que soit** = *whatever*
   Remember when using the word 'Quel' there must be agreement with the noun it qualifies. In this example, quelles is in the feminine plural to agree with the word circonstances which is a feminine plural noun. Soit must also be in the plural: soit-soient.
   Il faut faire en sorte que les gens malades soient traités avec compassion quelles que soient les circonstances.
   We must do what we can in order that sick people are treated with compassion, whatever the circumstances.

3. **Il y a une pression sur les épaules de** = *there is pressure put on the shoulders of...*
   Il y une pression sur les épaules des médecins de trouver des guérisons pour les gens.
   There is pressure put on the shoulders of doctors to find cures for people.

4. **Afin de** = *in order to* **(normally followed by a verb in the infinitive)**
   Je fais du sport afin de garder la ligne.
   I do sport in order to stay in good shape.

5. **Avoir lieu** = *to take place*
   The verb avoir must be put into the tense that you would like to write in eg. La boum a eu lieu hier soir – the party took place yesterday night.

   L'assemblée mondiale de l'Organisation Mondiale de la Santé a lieu tous les ans à Genève en Suisse.
   The general assembly of the World Health Organisation takes place every year, in Geneva, Switzerland.

6. **Être chargé de** = *to be responsible for*
   Le Ministre de la Santé en Irlande est chargé du fonctionnement de notre système de santé.
   The health minister in Ireland is responsible for operating our health system.

7. **Prendre de l'ampleur** = *to spread or to grow in size*
   Remember that the verb « Prendre » must be correctly conjugated into the tense required.
   Le taux d'incidence du SIDA prend de l'ampleur surtout en Afrique.
   The level of incidence of AIDS is spreading in Africa.

8. **Je ne supporte pas** = *I do not tolerate*
   Il faut avouer que je ne supporte pas une telle pratique.
   I must admit that I do not tolerate such a practice.

9. **À mon avis** = *in my opinion*
   À mon avis, les enfants aujourd'hui mènent des vies trop sédentaires.
   In my opinion, children today lead lives which are too sedentary.

10. **Il faut faire face à la réalité** = *we must face up to reality*
    De nos jours, il faut faire face à la réalité ; le gouvernement ne fait rien pour aider les toxicomanes.
    Nowadays, we must face up to reality; the government is doing nothing to help drug addicts.

Dix expressions authentiques et ludiques

1. Trouver chaussure à son pied = *to find what one needs or to meet the perfect match*
2. Jeter son dévolu = *to make a decisive choice*
3. Être médusé = *to be very surprised or dumbstruck*
4. Coûter un bras = *to cost a lot of money*
5. Un cheval de Troie = *a trap*
6. Prendre le train onze / le train onze / le train d'onze / le train d'onze heures = *to walk*
7. La huitième merveille du monde = *something absolutely remarkable or surprising*
8. C'est de l'hébreu / du chinois / de l'iroquois = *it's double dutch*
9. Un violon d'Ingres = *a hobby*
10. Courir / taper sur le système / le haricot = *to annoy or exasperate someone / to get on someone's nerves*

CHAPITRE 9

La technologie

Aural Section

A — La technologie moderne

Français	Anglais	How to pronounce
la technologie	technology	tek-nol-oh-jee
depuis	since /for	de-pwee
indispensable	vital	an-diss-pon-sabl
la livraison	the delivery	la leave-ray-zon
les réseaux	networks	lay rey-zoh

Écoutez et puis remplissez les blancs:

La technologie _____ a été définie par _____, particulièrement par le PC qui est devenu _____ depuis la deuxième _____ des années 80. Aujourd'hui, l'ordinateur portable a remplacé le PC. Le logiciel est la force _____ derrière ceci et a rendu l'ordinateur indispensable dans ___ vie. Nos communications sont établies à _____ de l'ordinateur. La télévision, la téléphonie et la radio sont numérisées. Les compagnies traditionnelles postales et de livraison _____ des ordinateurs pour aider leurs personnels et clients. Nos voitures ont des éléments éléctroniques _____, généralement sans que nous le sachions. Les _____ de signalisation et les panneaux de message au bord des routes sont informatisés. La technologie moderne nous a donné ____ des ordinateurs. Personellement je ne pourrais pas m'en passer ! Il _____ que la plupart de jeunes, sont membres des _____ sociaux tel que Facebook. Ils sont attirés par ce phénomène _____. Les enfants savent utiliser un ordinateur avec une connaissance presque enracinée ! L'internet est un réseau de communication et d'information sans _____. Mais attention, il y a des _____ et des contres. Il nous incombe d'instruire les jeunes aux risques _____ à ces réseaux. Il ne faut pas oublier qu'un écran ne pourrait jamais _____ le contacte humain.

Bonne Chance !

B La nano-technologie

Français	Anglais	How to pronounce
une discipline	*a subject*	oone diss-sea-pleen
moléculaire	*molecular*	mo-lek-queue-lair
une tête d'épingle	*a pinhead*	oone tet day-pangl
inéluctable	*inevitable*	an-el-luck-tabl
entièrement	*completely*	on-tea-air-mon

Listen then answer the following questions:

1. When did nano-technology start?
2. What is the principle of nano-technology based on?
3. Give one example of how nano-technology is used in medicine.
4. What danger does nano-technology pose?

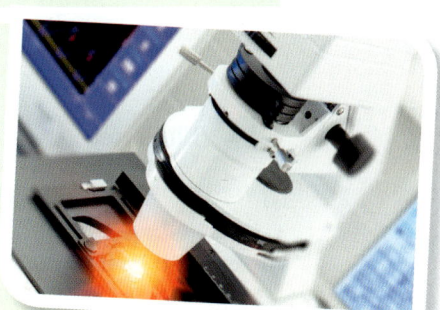

C Les portables

Français	Anglais	How to pronounce
les données	*data, information*	lay dun-nay
peuplé	*populated*	pup-lay
au courant	*to be aware or informed*	oh coor-ron
judiciaire	*judicial, legal*	jew-diss-see-air
clapoter	*to tap*	cla-po-tay
un forfait	*a flat fee*	an for-fay
illimité	*unlimited*	ee-lim-ee-tay
meilleur	*better*	may-er

Listen to the article then answer the following questions:

1. The article mentions 8 applications of a mobile phone. Name three of them.
    (a) _____
    (b) _____
    (c) _____
2. How has mobile technology helped in judicial cases?
3. According to Jeanne, what is the major advantage of mobile phones?
4. For what does Jeanne use her mobile phone?

Chapitre 9 La technologie

5. Paul gives a number of reasons why he does not like using mobile phones. Name two of them.
6. What for Lucie, is the best advantage of having a bill-pay phone?
7. Does Lucie have to be connected to the internet to listen to her music?

D L'internet

Français	Anglais	How to pronounce
un centre d'intérêt	a centre of interest	an sont dan-ter-ray
une occasion	an opportunity	oone oh-cazz-yon
éveiller	to awaken	ay-vey-ay
intellectuelle	intellectual	an-tell-lek-tue-el
synthétiser	to synthesise	san-tay-tea-zay

Listen to the following people speak about the pros and cons of the internet, then answer the questions below.

1. When does Jennifer spend a lot of time on the internet? _to connect on the week-end_
2. Give two examples of how Jennifer uses the internet. _to listen to music, to watch videos._
3. Complete the following:

    C'est _vrai_ que l'internet occupe une _place_ importante dans la vie des jeunes. L'internet _est_ devenu un véritable _phénomène_ social. Cependant, il éveille les _apprehensions_ de certains parents et éducateurs. Ceux-ci le considèrent _comme_ un danger qui menace les enfants et les jeunes. Les jeunes passent indifféremment d'un _site_ à l'autre sans _objectif_ précis. Un grand nombre d'entre eux veillent _tard_ dans la nuit pour naviguer sur des sites de _partage_ l'Internet est devenu pour ces jeunes une obsession _ou_ une drogue.

4. Write down whether or not M. Thibault made the following statements:

Statement	Number
A The internet causes intellectual laziness.	1
B Students never print the complete document.	X
C Internet research has dreadful consequences for study.	2
D Students read more thanks to the internet.	X

E La télévision

Français	Anglais	How to pronounce
jamais	*never*	jah-may
évasion	*escape*	ay-vaz-yon
franchement	*frankly or honestly*	fronch-mon
la vie quotidienne	*daily life*	la vee co-tid-dee-en

Listen to the extract and then write down the order in which the following were said:

Statement	Number
I never miss an episode as it is my only escape this year	
television has become digital	
but on top of this	
it really annoys me!	
A there is nothing better than lounging in front of one's favourite programme.	12
I love this series as it is really entertaining	
honestly, technology has changed everything in daily life	
B I am following a great series	3
my uncle has a smart television	
C television is a good way of relaxing	12

F Le commerce en ligne

Français	Anglais	How to pronounce
la crise	*the crisis*	la creeze
grimper	*to climb*	gram-pay
auparavant	*before now*	oh-para-von
méfiant	*wary*	mef-fee-on
quasiment	*practically*	caz-zee-mon

Remplissez les blancs:

Le _____ en ligne ne connaît pas de _____. La Fédération de l'e-commerce et de ___ vente à distance présente un _____ très positif. Les achats sur le web grimpent ____ les jours. Les gens, auparavant méfiants _____ plus confiance aujourd'hui et les achats se font très _____. C'est très pratique de pouvoir rester à la maison et de faire ses emplettes, surtout si vous avez des enfants ou si vous êtes très occupé. Les sites commerciaux ont pris des _____ de sécurité et c'est quasiment impossible d'accéder à vos détails personnels. Cependant il faut que vous _____ vigilants. L'e-commerce est _____ tellement important dans la vie quotidienne qu'on se demande comment les gens faisaient _____. Si vous habitez dans un petit patelin loin de tout, vous pouvez avoir _____ à des boutiques qui vendent des produits non présent chez _____. Les jeunes commandent des affaires très _____ sur Internet et souvent c'est vraiment moins cher. Une chose est certaine, l'e-commerce reste en forte _____ malgré la crise.

Est-ce que vous étes quelqu'un qui fait des achats sur le canapé ou est-ce que vous préfèrez sortir et toucher la marchandise avant d'acheter? Écoutez trois personnes qui donnent leur opinion sur ce sujet.

1. What does Madeleine find practical?
2. What day does she do her shopping?
3. Why does Loic not trust the internet?
4. Why does Jean-Claude think that the internet is a good idea?
5. What does he say about delivery of items or products?

G Leaving Cert Ordinary Level 2009 Section 1

Français	Anglais	How to pronounce
ancien	old or former	on-see-en
depuis	for / since	de-pwee
ensuite	then	on-sweet
directement	directly	dee-rek-te-mon

Three French people, Lucie, Raymond and Clara, tell us what they do with their old mobile phones. You will hear the interview three times: first right through, then in three segments with pauses, and finally right through again.

1. To whom did Lucie give her old mobile phone?
    (a) Her sister.
    (b) Her brother.
    (c) Her cousin.
    (d) Her friend.
2. What does Raymond generally do with his old mobile phones?
3. How many mobile phones has Clara had?
    (a) Three or four.
    (b) Five or six.
    (c) Seven or eight.
    (d) Nine or ten.

4. What does Clara do with her old phones now?
    (a) She keeps them in her office.
    (b) She gives them away.
    (c) She recycles them.
    (d) She puts them in the bin.

H Les faits divers

Français	Anglais	How to pronounce
accéder	*to access*	ak-say-day
l'affaire du siècle	*the bargain of the century*	la-fair do see-ekl
fabricant	*manufacturer*	fab-ree-con
les enjeux	*the stakes*	lays on-juh

Article 1.
1. La dame dans le premier article vient de fêter quelle anniversaire ?
2. Pourquoi elle est si contente ?

Article 2.
1. Les télévisions smart coûtent combien selon le deuxième article ?
2. Pourquoi Monsieur Dupont n'a payé que €1,00 ?

Article 3.
1. Combien coûte le smartphone fabriqué par un fournisseur chinois ?

Oral Section – *Let's Get Talking*
Ten common questions on the subject of technology

Français	Anglais	How to pronounce
Avez-vous un portable ?	*Do you have a mobile phone?*	ah-vay voo an por-tabl?
À votre avis, quelle est la meilleure invention des dernières années ?	*In your opinion, what has been the best invention in recent years?*	ah votr ah-vee kel ay la may-er an-vonce-yon say der-nee-er an-nay?
Est-ce que vous faites des achats en ligne ?	*Do you make purchases on-line?*	esse-kuh voo fet days ah-shah on-lean?
Est-ce que vous utilisez l'internet chez vous ?	*Do you use the internet at home?*	esse-kuh voo you-til-lee-zay lan-ter-net shay voo?
Est-ce que vous aimez regarder la télévision ?	*Do you like watching television?*	esse-kuh vooz em-may re-gar-day la tellay-viz-yon?

Est-ce que vous avez une tablette ?	Do you have a tablet?	esse-kuh vooz ah-vay oone tab-lett
Que pensez vous des e-books ?	What do you think of e-books?	kuh pon-say voo de e-books?
Que pensez vous de la télé-réalité ?	What do you think of reality TV?	kuh pon-say voo de la tellay ray-al-lee-tay?
Est-ce que vous téléchargez la musique ?	Do you download music?	esse-kuh voo tellay-char-jay la musique?
Est-ce que votre école utilise des tableaux blancs interactifs ?	Does your school use interactive white boards?	esse-kuh votr ay-cull you-teel-ease day tab-low blon an-ter-ak-teef?

Dix questions et réponses possibles sur la technologie

1. **Avez-vous un portable ?**

   Oui, j'ai un portable et je le trouve très pratique surtout si je veux contacter quelqu'un en cas d'urgence. Sinon, c'est également utile de pouvoir regarder des clips sur YouTube ou simplement de télécharger des jeux ou des petits programmes me permettant d'accéder à des fonctions ludiques ou informatives.

   Yes, I have a mobile phone and I find it very useful especially if I want to contact someone urgently. If not, it is equally useful to be able to watch clips on YouTube or simply to download games or apps which allow me to access games or informative sites.

2. **À votre avis, quelle est la meilleure invention des dernières années ?**

   Pour moi, il va sans dire que la meilleure invention des dernières années était le/la/les *(insert the invention of your choice here)*. Cette invention a changé la façon dans laquelle nous vivons.

   For me, it goes without saying that the best invention in recent years was the (insert the invention of your choice here). This invention has changed the way in which we live.

3. **Est-ce que vous faites des achats enligne ?**

   Je fais des achats de temps en temps. Je n'ai pas ma propre carte de crédit et il faut que j'utilise celle de ma mère. J'ai une limite de €50 et je ne la dépasse jamais. J'achète des fringues ou du maquillage ou des billets pour les concerts.

   I make purchases from time to time. I don't have my own credit card so I have to use my mother's. I have a limit of €50 and I never go over it. I buy clothes or make-up or concert tickets.

   Non, je n'ai pas le droit d'acheter des produits sur l'internet. Mes parents ne font pas confiance aux commerces en ligne. Comme ils peuvent être bêtes les parents ! Tous mes amis font des achats en ligne et souvent ils font des affaires !

   No, I am not allowed buy any products on the internet. My parents don't trust on-line businesses. How stupid parents can be! All my friends buy on line and they often get bargains.

4. **Est-ce que vous utilisez l'internet chez vous ?**
   Oui, je me sers de l'internet mais c'est trop facile d'être détourné par les réseaux sociaux comme Facebook ou Twitter. Normalement je commence par faire des recherches sur des matières qui concernent l'école mais cela tourne vite et je finis par papoter avec les amis.
   Yes, I use the internet but it is too easy to be distracted by social networking sites like Facebook or Twitter. Usually I start by reseaching subjects which concern school but this changes quickly and I end up chatting to my friends.

5. **Est-ce que vous aimez regarder la télévision ?**
   La télévision est un bon moyen de se défouler après une journée fatigante à l'école. Il ne peut rien y avoir de mieux que de traîner devant une bonne émission. J'aime bien être seul quand je regarde la télévision car mon frère monopolise la télécommande et il zappe sans cesse. Comme il peut être exaspérant !
   Television is a good way of chilling out after a tiring day at school. There is nothing better than lazing about watching a good programme. I really like to be alone when I watch television because my brother hogs the remote and changes channels constantly. How annoying he can be!

6. **Est-ce que vous avez une tablette ?**
   Non, je n'ai pas de tablette. Tout le monde dit que la tablette est mieux que l'ordinateur portable mais je n'en suis pas persuadé(e). J'aime mieux clapoter sur un clavier. Je n'aime pas le fait que tout est fait sur un écran tactile.
   No, I don't have a tablet. Everyone says that the tablet is better than the laptop, but I am not convinced. I prefer to tap on a keyboard. I don't like the fact that everything is done on a touch-screen.

   J'ai reçu une tablette pour mon anniversaire et je peux vous dire que pour moi, c'est la meilleure invention jusqu'ici ! Je peux tout faire sur ma tablette et elle est tellement légère. J'amène ma tablette en classe et je prends des notes. Je n'en ai plus besoin d'un stylo !
   I received a tablet for my birthday and I can tell you that for me, it is the best invention yet! I can do everything on my tablet and it is so light. I bring my tablet to class and I take notes. I no longer need a pen!

7. **Que pensez vous de ebooks ?**
   Les e-books ou les livres numériques deviennent de plus en plus courants. Ma mère a un Kindle à la maison et elle télécharge des livres très souvent. Moi, je préfère lire des vrais livres. Je pense que les livres numériques sont mieux pour l'environnement et que dans vingt ans, les livres vont tous être numériques.
   E-books or electronic books are becoming more and more common. My mother has a Kindle at home and she downloads books very often. Me, I prefer to read real books. I think that e-books are better for the environment and that in twenty years, books will all be digitised.

8. **Que pensez vous de la télé-réalité ?**

La télé-réalité est un phenomène extraordinaire de nos jours surtout depuis la diffusion de Big Brother en 1999. Ce genre de télévision est très attirant pour les spectateurs car il n'y a pas d'acteurs professionels, juste les gens de tous les jours. La télé-réalité n'est pas chère à transmettre, ni à produire. Cela dit, ces émissions peuvent avoir une mauvaise influence sur les jeunes, surtout quand on voit des gens qui boivent trop.

Reality TV is an extraordinary phenomenon nowadays since the transmission of Big Brother in 1999. This type of television is very attractive for viewers because there are no professional actors, just everyday people. Reality TV is not expensive to air or to produce. This said, these programmes can have a bad influence on young people, especially when we see people who drink too much.

9. **Est-ce que vous téléchargez la musique ?**

Oui pour être franche il faut que je dise la vérité. Je télécharge la musique comme tous mes amis. Quand la musique téléchargée est devenue populaire, beaucoup ont enregistré la musique disponible en dehors des réseaux de distribution traditionnels. Maintenant, le marché pour télécharger la musique est mieux organisé. Pour les jeunes, c'est un moyen d'avoir une grande collection de musique, et comme disait une copine à ce sujet « Contrairement à voler une pomme dans un marché public, je ne me ferai jamais prendre. »

Yes, to be honest I have to tell the truth. I download music like all my friends. When downloading music became popular a lot of people recorded music which was available outside the traditional distribution networks. Now, the market for downloading music is better organised. For young people, it is a way of having a big music collection, and as a friend of mine said regarding this, 'Unlike stealing an apple in a market, I will never be caught'.

10. **Est-ce que votre école utilise des tableaux blancs interactifs ?**

Non, pas encore, mais quelle bonne idée ! Je sais que les tableaux noirs/des whiteboards interactifs sont connectés à l'internet via un ordinateur sophistiqué. Il est particulièrement utile dans les matières tels que les mathématiques, les science physiques, les sciences sociales et les langues. La salle de classe interactive apporte un éventail de ressources. C'est une façon de s'assurer que le matériel couvert en classe est tout à fait à jour. Les tableaux interactifs sont une invention formidable dans les établissements scolaires. Si un étudiant est malade, il peut venir voir le professeur avec sa clé USB et faire une copie de l'information requise. Seul problème pour nous les étudiants – plus d'excuses !

No, not yet, but what a great idea! I know that black board/interactive white boards are connected to the internet via a sophisticated computer. It is particularly useful in subjects such as maths, biology, social science and languages. The interactive classroom brings a wide range of resources. It is a way of ensuring that the material covered in class is completely up to date. Interactive boards are a great invention in schools. If a student is ill, they can come to see the teacher with their USB key and make a copy of all the requisite information. Only problem for us students – no more excuses!

Le Vocabulaire Essentiel

Français	Anglais	How to pronounce
flambant neuf	brand spanking new	flam-bon nuff
séduire	to charm	sed-dweer
brancher	to plug in	bron-shay
généré par ordinateur	computer generated	jen-ner-ray par or-din-nah-tur
suivre le mouvement	to jump on the bandwagon	sweev le moov-mon
la conception assistée par ordinateur	computer aided design	la con-seps-yon ah-cyst-tay par or-din-nah-tur
les images de synthèse	computer graphics	lays ee-maje de san-tez
la compétence en informatique	computer literacy	la com-pay-tonce on an-for-ma-teek
le courrier électronique	e-mail	le coor-ree-ay el-ek-tron-neek
le raccordement	connection	le rah-cord-deh-mon
le bouquet	a package	le boo-kay
la mise à jour	the update	la meez-ah-joor
le réseau	the network	le ray-zoh
un atout	an asset, a trump card	an ah-too
la technologie de pointe	state of the art technology	la teck-nol-oh-jee de pwant
la carte à puce	smart card	la cart-ah-poose
l'essor	the growth	less-sor
l'ère informatique	the computer age	lair an-for-ma-teek
un domaine de recherche	a field of research	an do-men de reh-sherch
envisager	to envisage	on-viz-zah-jay
la taille minuscule des atomes	the miniscule size of atoms	la tie min-iss-cule days ah-tum
un outil	a tool	an oo-tee
interagir	to interact	an-ter-rah-jeer
observer	to observe	ob-zer-vay
l'invention	the invention	lan-vonce-yon
le développement	the development	le deh-vel-lope-mon
un objet de très petit taille	a really tiny object	an ob-jay de tray pet-tee tie
faramineux	surprising	fara-mee-neuh
inéluctable	inevitable	an-el-luck-tabl
outrepasser	to exceed	ut-tre-pass-ay
les nanoparticules	nano particles	lay nano-par-tee-cool
la mécanique	mechanics	la meh-can-neek

Chapitre 9 La technologie

l'optique	*optics*	lop-teek
l'échelle	*the scale*	lay-shel
un dispositif	*a device*	an diss-poze-zeh-teef
la téléphonie mobile	*mobile telephony*	la tellay-fon-nee moh-beel
un moyen de télécommunication	*a method of telecommunication*	an moy-en de tellay-com-mune-nee-cass-yon
les paramètres	*the settings*	lay para-mettr
tracer des mobiles volés	*to trace stolen phones*	tra-say day moh-beel vul-lay
un code de déverrouillage	*unlocking code*	an cud de de-ver-rue-aje
sans fil	*wireless*	sawn feel
les kits mains-libres de voiture	*hands-free kit for cars*	lay kit man-leebr de vwa-toor
être au mode veille	*to be on stand-by*	et-re oh mud vay
la sonnerie	*the ring tone*	la sun-ner-ree
le service de messagerie	*messaging service*	le sir-veece de meh-saj-ger-ree
un appel entrant	*an incoming call*	an ah-pel on-tron
le téléphone fixe	*the land-line*	le tellay-fon fix
s'interconnecter	*to interconnect*	san-ter-con-neck-tay
compatible	*compatible*	com-pat-teeb
la qualité de réception	*la reception quality*	la cal-lee-tay de re-ceps-yon
un format de poche	*pocket-sized*	an for-ma de poche
l'utilisateur	*the user*	loo-tee-lise-ah-tur
la voix	*the voice*	la voie
le smart phone / le téléphone intelligent	*smart phone*	le smart fon/ le tellay-fon an-tell-lee-jon
l'appareil téléphonique	*telephone device*	lap-par-rye tellay-fon-neek
la page d'accueil	*the homepage*	la page dak-coy
la toile, le web	*the world wide web*	la twall/le web
naviguer dans le web	*to surf the web*	nav-vee-gay don le web
le fournisseur d'accès	*the Internet provider*	le foor-nee-sir dak-say
télécharger un document	*to download a document*	tellay-shar-jay an docu-mon
se connecter à l'internet	*to connect to the internet*	se con-neck-tay ah lan-ter-net
le moteur de recherche	*the search engine*	le mo-tur de ray-sherch
un logiciel	*software*	an lo-jiss-see-el
sauvegarder des données	*saving data*	sauf-gar-day day don-nay
le disque dur	*the hard disk*	le disk dure
l'écran	*the screen*	lay-cron
le clavier	*the keyboard*	le cla-vee-ay

le mot de passe	*the password*	le mo-de-pass
le mode de fonctionnement hors ligne	*offline functioning*	le mud de funk-see-on-mon oar leen
le mode de fontionnnement en ligne	*online functioning*	le mud de funk-see-on-mon on leen
cliquer sur un lien	*to click on a link*	click-ay sur an lee-en
la souris	*the mouse*	la sue-ree
ouvrir/fermer une fenêtre	*to open / close a window*	oov-rear/fer-may oone fen-netr
un ordinateur	*a computer*	an/or-din-na-tur
émettre	*to transmit*	ay-metr
les émissions	*programmes*	lays eh-miss-yon
les spots publicitaires	*ad breaks*	lay spot poob-liss-see-tair
le contenu	*contents*	le con-ten-nu
les ondes	*waves*	lays ond
un réseau câblé	*a cable network*	an ray-zoh cab-lay
le petit écran	*the TV*	le pet-tee ay-cron
une antenne parabolique	*a satellite dish*	oone on-ten para-bol-leak
regarder la télévision	*to watch TV*	re-gar-day la tellay-viz-yon
se détendre	*to relax*	se de-tondr
la zapette	*the remote control (familiar language)*	la zap-pet
la télécommande	*the remote control*	la tellay-com-mond
le modem	*the modem*	le mo-dem
un brevet	*a patent*	an brev-vay
un tube cathodique	*a cathode ray tube*	an toob cat-to-deek
des moyen électromagnétiques	*electromagnetic means*	day moy-en el-lek-tro-man-nyet-teek
la reproduction de l'image	*the reproduction of the image*	la re-pro-ducks-yon de lee-maje
numérique	*digital*	new-mer-reek
un téléviseur à écran large	*a wide-screen TV*	an tellay-viz-er ah ay-cron large
rebobiner	*to rewind*	re-bob-bee-nay
un DVD	*a DVD*	an day-vay-day
un faisceau	*a beam or ray*	an fay-soh
une quantité d'œuvres	*a quantity of works*	oon kwan-tee-tay dov-re
télécharger illégalement	*to download illegally*	tellay-shar-jay ee-lay-gal-mon
un revenu	*an income*	an re-ven-nu
un bandit de la musique	*a music thief*	an bon-dee de la musique

Chapitre 9 **La technologie**

la polémique	the controversy	la po-le-meek
fouiller	to search, to go through	fwee-ay
chercher à	try to	sher-shay
un groupe	a group	an group
un chanteur	a singer	an shawn-ter
interdire	to forbid	an-ter-deer
tourner en boucle	to play music on a continuous loop	toor-nay on boucl
prendre de l'ampleur	to grow in popularity	prond-re de lom-pleur
un son pourri	a rotten sound (familiar language)	an sohn poo-ree
le piratage	pirating	le peer-ra-taje
faire confiance à quelqu'un	to trust someone	fair con-fee-once ah kel-can
l'investissement	the investment	lan-ves-tiss-mon

Dix constructions clés sur la technologie

1. **En plus = *on top of that***
   La technologie nous aide dans la vie et en plus, la compétence en informatique est un atout pour le marché du travail.
   Technology helps us in life and, on top of that, computer literacy is an asset in the labour market.

2. **C'est dégoûtant = *it is disgusting or distasteful***
   C'est dégoûtant de voir comment les jeunes passent la plupart de leurs vacances à jouer sur les consoles de jeux.
   It is disgusting to see how young people spend most of their holidays playing game consoles.

3. **Sans aucun doute = *without any doubt***
   Sans aucun doute, la technologie de pointe a fait beaucoup pour la médecine.
   Without any doubt, state-of-the-art technology has done a lot for medicine.

4. **Je mettrais en place = *I would put in place***
   Si j'étais à la tête de Facebook, je mettrais en place des mesures plus efficaces pour sensibiliser les jeunes aux dangers liés à l'internet.
   If I was in charge of Facebook I would put in place more effective measures to alert young people to the dangers attached to the internet.

5. **Il nous incombe tous de + infinitive = *it is up to us all to***
   Il nous incombe tous de faire attention.
   It is up to all of us to be careful.

6. **Pourtant = *however***
   C'est facile de télécharger illégalement la musique, et pourtant, ceci a causé un problème pour l'industrie de musique. L'achat traditionnel de la musique est en régression.
   It is easy to download music illegally, however this has caused a problem for the music industry. The traditional purchase of music is in decline.

7. **Ne + verb + que = *only* eg: elle ne parle que le français = *she only speaks French***
   Tu ne peux utiliser l'internet que pendant le weekend.
   You can only use the internet at the weekend.

8. **Le problème réside dans le fait que = *the root of the problem is that...***
   Je n'arrive pas à ouvrir mon courrier électronique. Le problème réside dans le fait que le raccordement est en panne.
   I am not able to open my e-mail. The root of the problem is that the connection is broken.

9. **Il est devenu carrément + adjective = *it has become absolutely...***
   Il est devenu carrément impossible de trouver un travail sans une bonne connaissance de l'informatique.
   It has become absolutely impossible to find work without a good knowledge of computers.

10. **C'est la responsabilité du gouvernement de résoudre cette crise = *it is the responsibility of the government to resolve this crisis***
    (Change 'government' to any other noun)
    C'est la responsabilité du gouvernement de résoudre cette crise. Nous en avons ras-le-bol!
    It is the responsibility of the government to resolve this crisis. We have had enough!

Dix expressions authentiques et ludiques

1. Par acquit de conscience = *to set one's mind at ease*
2. Ça lui fait une belle jambe = *a fat lot of good that will do him/ a useful piece of information (ironic)*
3. De bon / mauvais aloi = *to be of good / bad quality*
4. Faire table rase = *to go back to zero*
5. Un été indien = *an indian summer*
6. Franchir le Rubicon = *to cross the Rubicon / to take a decisive and irreversible step / to make a decision and assume the consequences*
7. Fumer une sèche / une clope = *to smoke a cigarette*
8. Lâcher la proie pour l'ombre = *to turn your back on something real in favour of an intangible thing, a false hope*
9. De la bouillie pour les chats = *spoiled work / a badly written, incomprehensible piece of work / something that is completely useless*
10. Être gonflé / Ne pas manquer d'air = *reckless, rash, audacious*

CHAPITRE 10 — Les problèmes sociaux

Aural Section

A La pauvreté, la drogue et l'émigration

Nous parlons avec trois jeunes qui mentionnent ce que sont pour eux les problèmes sociaux qui les touchent.

Français	Anglais	How to pronounce
un problème	a problem	an prob-lem
les pays de l'ouest	western countries	lay pay-ee de loest
meilleure (f)	better	may-eur
ainsi	thus	ann-sea
afin de	in order to	ah-fan de

Écoutez puis répondez aux questions suivantes:

1. Selon Christine, comment est-ce qu'on peut sortir de la pauvreté?
2. Ainsi, je _____ qu'il est indispensable d'offrir les _____ nécessaires et de fournir à tous suffisamment d'options _____ de renforcer la _____ financière et l'autonomie ___ chacun.
3. Selon Jean-Paul, quel est le problème qui touche le plus de monde?
4. Comment est-ce que les gens débutent dans cette pratique?
5. Lucie dit que l'émigration est devenu le fléau de notre sociéte. Comment est-ce que Lucie est personnellement touchée?
6. Le gouvernement dit que les chiffres du registre diminuent. Selon Lucie, comment est-ce que cela est arrivé?

B Le jeu de hasard

Français	Anglais	How to pronounce
attirer	to attract	ah-teer-ray
potentiel	potential	po-ton-see-el
lier	to link or to connect	lee-ay
les conséquences	consequences	lay con-say-conce
occasionnel	occasional	oh-caze-zee-on-el
la dépendance	dependency	la day-pon-donce

Remplissez les blancs:

Le jeu de hasard est l'un des _____ importants types de détente et de _____ de nos jours. On est généralement attiré à ces activités ____ les gains potentiels et le _____ d'excitation qu'on obtient à y participer. Les jeux de hasard nous _____ cependant à lier notre gagne-pain au hasard, entraînant des conséquences qui _____ non seulement nous affecter nous-même, mais _____ notre famille également. Je pense qu'il est important de savoir _____ s'arrêter, d'utiliser ces _____ comme un divertissement occasionnel et de ne pas tomber dans le _____ de la dépendence.

C La discrimination raciale

Français	Anglais	How to pronounce
la discrimination	discrimination	la diss-crim-min-nass-yon
malheureusement	unfortunately	mal-er-reuz-mon
l'intensité	the intensity	lan-ton-see-tay
les préjugés	prejudice	lay prey-ju-jay
remédier	to resolve	re-maid-dee-ay
bénéficier	to benefit	bennay-feece-see-ay

Chapitre 10 Les problèmes sociaux

Trouvez la phrase française pour les phrases anglaises suivantes:

Anglais	Français
racial discrimination belongs to the past	
it still exists	
the intensity of their prejudices	
their country of origin	
the travelling community	
it is time to recognise	
in order to	
obvious	
an attack on the principle of equality	
equal rights	

D Les mannequins de taille zéro

Français	Anglais	How to pronounce
les mannequins	models	lay man-nay-kan
mince	slim	mance
les corps	bodies	lay cor
réaliser	to understand	ray-al-lee-zay
les défilés	a parade or catwalk	lay day-fee-lay

Write down the order in which you hear the following phrases:

Phrase	Number
the girls on cat walks and in magazines are not real beings	
the twisted world of fashion	
modelling agencies hire very young girls	
a representation of beauty	
this is not reality	
size zero models feel pressurised into following very severe diets	
Victoria Beckham is a 39-year-old woman	
girls at school	
airbrush	
putting their health in danger	

Bonne Chance !

E La peine de mort

Français	Anglais	How to pronounce
le signe	the sign	le seen
prodiguer	to dispense	pro-dee-gay
l'abolition	the abolition	labo-liss-yon
en particulier	in particular	on par-tick-queue-lee-ay
un ralliement	an assembly or a rallying	an rye-mon

Expliquer les chiffres et les dates:

Chiffre	Explication
1981	
36ème	
2002	
108	
189	
90%	
4	

F Le cyber-harcèlement

Français	Anglais	How to pronounce
sensible	sensitive / susceptible	sawn-see-bl
l'harcèlement	bullying	lar-sel-mon
un phénomène	a phenomenon	an fen-no-men
les réseaux sociaux	social networks	lay reh-zo so-see-oh
la réclusion	imprisonment	la reh-cluz-yon
une enquête	a survey / investigation	oone on-kett

Rémplissez les blancs dans cet article avec les verbes qui manquent:

Avez-vous déjà eu le sentiment que quelqu'un vous _____ sans _____ pourquoi? Sur l'internet, on ne ____ jamais être sûr de qui nous _____ et quand. Nous _____ tous ouverts et sensibles au harcèlement en ligne. Le cyber-harcèlement ____ un nouveau mode de harcèlement né des nouvelles technologies, qui fait de plus en plus _____ de lui. Ce phénomène, qui n'____ autre qu'une forme d'agression _____ par la réception répétée de messages par SMS ou sur le Net (MSN, e-mail, réseaux sociaux.) Le cyber-harcèlement ____ contraire à la loi et peut _____ des pénalités jusqu'à la réclusion. Ceux qui _____ du cyber harcèlement _____ souvent ceux qui _____ le besoin de _____ une autre personne. Si le harcèlement _____ et dans les cas sérieux, la police peut être avertie. À cette fin des «preuves» _____ toutefois nécessaires pour que celle-ci puisse _____ son enquête. C'est pourquoi vos enfants _____ au cas-où, _____ à _____ les messages problématiques.

G Les célébrités

Français	Anglais	How to pronounce
les célébrités	celebrities	lay sell-leb-ree-tay
à travers	through	ah tra-vair
un niveau	a level	an nee-vo
la renommée	reputation	la reh-no-may

Trouvez l'expression française pour les phrases suivantes :

Anglais	Français
in certain cases	
to be in the limelight	
a public figure	
who attracts attention	
a level of interest	
the reason for their fame	
an exceptional act	
there are also celebrities	
a certain domain	
the world of dance	

H La puissance de la publicité

Français	Anglais	How to pronounce
la puissance	the power	la pwee-sonce
une campagne	a campaign	oone cam-pan
créer	to create	cray-ay
de fil en aiguille	gradually	de feel on ay-gwee
les goûts	tastes	lay goo
les bannières	banners	lay ban-nee-air
j'apprécie	I appreciate	jah-pre-see

Answer the questions below.

1. Les entreprises de publicité savent tenter qui ?
2. Donnez un exemple d'une marque réprésenté par Saatchi & Saatchi ?
3. Qu'est-ce que votre panier réprésente pour les boîtes de publicité ?
4. Quel est le gagne-pain des entreprises publicitaires ?
5. La publicité en ligne permet aux webmasters de faire quoi exactement ?
6. Pourquoi est-ce que la publicité en ligne est souvent très gênante pour ceux qui sont en ligne ?

I Le clonage

Français	Anglais	How to pronounce
les cellules	cells	lay sell-yule
soigner	to take care of	swan-yay
inévitable	inevitable	in-ev-vee-tabl
la mutilation	the mutilation	la mu-til-ass-yon
sciemment	deliberately	see-ay-mon
un vieillissement	ageing	an vee-ace-mon
infructueux	fruitless	an-frook-chuh
viable	viable or feasible	vee-abl

Answer the questions below

1. What is the aim of human cloning research?
2. What is the intention of some doctors in the world?
3. How does cloning of mammals usually end?
4. In what year was Dolly the sheep cloned?
5. How many attempts were necessary before succeeding in getting a viable clone?

J L'expérimentation animale

Français	Anglais	How to pronounce
affreux	*awful*	af-ruh
les réglements	*regulations*	lay reg-le-mon
les fins	*purposes*	lay fann
se maquiller	*to put on make-up*	se mack-key-ay
martyriser	*to torture*	mar-tir-ree-zay
guérir	*to cure*	gay-reer

Remplissez les blancs dans cet article avec les verbes qui manquent:

Faire des tests ____ les animaux. C'est _____ Je pense qu'il faut que le gouvernement fasse quelque chose afin de _____ en place les réglements concernant cette pratique. C'est _____ de se cacher derrière des compagnies de _____ qui ont des façades élégantes. La réalité est _____ autre chose. Les animaux sont utilisés pour des fins scientifiques. _____ matin des gens prennent des douches, se parfument, les femmes se maquillent et tous ces ____ utilisent des produits pour prendre soin de leur _____. Mais tous ces produits que nous utilisons pour nous rendre _____ et belles, comment ont-ils été faits? Pour la _____, des animaux ont été tués pour pouvoir _____ tous ces produits avant que nous le fassions nous-mêmes. Effectivement, tous ces _____ animaux innocents se font _____ par les compagnies qui fabriquent ces produits pour savoir s'ils sont _____ pour l'être humain. Beaucoup d'animaux meurent dans ____ laboratoires et cela fait empirer plus les problèmes, _____ grâce aux animaux on a trouvé des médicaments qui guérissent des maladies graves.

Oral Section – *Let's Get Talking*
Ten common questions on the subject of social issues

Français	Anglais	How to pronounce
Beaucoup vivent au seuil de pauvreté. Que pensez-vous?	*A lot of people live on the poverty line. What do you think?*	boo-coo veev oh soy de pauv-re-tay. kuh pon-say voo?
Y a-t-il beaucoup de problèmes sociaux en Irlande?	*Are there a lot of social problems in Ireland?*	ee-ah-teel boo-coo de pro-lem so-see-oh on ear-lond?
Quel est votre avis sur la situation économique en Irlande?	*What is your opinion about the economic situation in Ireland?*	kel ay votr avee sewer la sit-you-ass-yon ay-con-no-meek on ear-lond?
Après les études est-ce que vous avez l'intention de partir à l'étranger?	*After your studies, do you intend going abroad?*	ah-prey lays ay-tude esse-kuh vooz ah-vay lan-tonce-yon de par-teer ah lay-tron-jere
Que pensez vous de Facebook?	*What do you think of Facebook?*	kuh pon-say voo de Facebook?
La publicité est partout et très puissante. Que pensez-vous?	*Advertising is everywhere and is very powerful. What do you think?*	la pub-liss-see-tay ay par-too ay tray pwee-sawnt. kuh pon-say voo?
Est-ce que vous êtes pour ou contre la peine de mort?	*Are you for or against the death penalty?*	esse-kuh vooz et poor oo cont la pen de mor
Le problème de la drogue est répandu en Irlande. Qu'est-ce qu'on peut faire pour limiter ses dégâts?	*The drug problem is widespread in Ireland. What can we do to limit its damaging effects?*	le prob-lem de la drug ay re-pon-du on ear-lond. kess kon puh fair poor lim-mee-tay say de-ga?
Que feriez-vous pour améliorer le sort des immigrés clandestins?	*What would you do to improve the fate of illigal immigrants?*	kuh ferry-ay voo poor ah-melly-oar-ay le sor days im-mee-grey clon-dess-tan?
Le crime est en augmentation dans nos villes en Irlande. Est-ce que le gouvernment fait assez pour lutter contre les gangs criminels?	*Crime is rising in our cities in Ireland. Does the government do enough to fight against criminal gangs?*	le creem et on og-mon-tass-yon don no veel on ear-lond. Esse-kuh le goo-ver-ne-mon fay ah-say poor loo-tay cont lay gong crim-mee-nel?

Dix questions et réponses possibles sur les problèmes sociaux

1. **Beaucoup vivent au seuil de pauvreté. Que pensez-vous ?**
   Depuis la sévère récession qui a frappé l'Irlande en 2008, beaucoup d'irlandais ont basculé dans la pauvreté. Des milliers de personnes sont maintenant vulnérables et il y a maintenant des familles qui n'ont pas assez pour se nourrir ni se loger. C'est honteux et il incombe à notre gouvernement de régler cette situation précaire.
   Since the severe recession which hit Ireland in 2008, a lot of Irish people have fallen into poverty. Thousands of people are now vulnerable and there are families who do not have enough to feed or house themselves. It is shameful and it is up to our government to sort out this precarious situation.

2. **Y a-t-il beaucoup de problèmes sociaux en Irlande ?**
   Oui sans doute il existe pas mal de problèmes sociaux en Irlande. Pour les jeunes le chômage reste un problème préoccupant. Notre pays, déjà fragilisé par la crise dans la zone euro ne voit pas de solutions réelles. Les conditions difficiles poussent les manifestants dans les rues pour protester contre l'impossibilité de cette crise, mais personne ne peut trouver une solution. Je ne veux pas partir et quitter ma famille, mais je ne vois pas comment je peux faire autrement. Les banquiers ont détruit notre pays avec l'avarice et c'est à nous de trinquer.
   Yes without doubt, there exist quite a few social problems in Ireland. For young people, unemployment remains a worrying problem. Our country, which was already weakened by the euro-zone crisis, is not seeing any tangible solutions. The difficult conditions are pushing protesters out onto the streets to protest about the impossibility of this crisis, but no-one can find the answer. I do not want to leave my family but I do not see what else I can do. The bankers have destroyed our country with greed and it is up to us to carry the can.

3. **Quel est votre avis sur la situation économique en Irlande ?**
   Je suis très déçu(e) par la situation actuelle chez nous. La crise a touché de façon particulièrement brutale notre pays après l'éclatement de la bulle immobilière. Nous sommes placé sous la surveillance budgétaire de la troïka. Notre économie est dépendante des investissements étrangers et des exportations. Je ne sais pas comment les choses vont tourner, mais j'espère que les mesures prises par le gouvernement vont améliorer notre situation.
   I am very disappointed by the current situation here. The crisis has affected our country in a singularly brutal manner after the property bubble burst. We have been placed under budgetary surveillance by the troïka. Our economy is dependant on foreign investment and exports. I do not know how things are going to pan out, but I hope that the measures taken by the government will improve our situation.

4. **Après les études est-ce que vous avez l'intention de partir à l'étranger ?**
   J'ai l'intention d'aller vivre dans un autre pays pour quelques années après ma licence. Je pense que c'est une bonne idée de partir et de voir comment vivent les autres. J'aimerais habiter au Canada. Je peux toujours visiter les États-Unis et au moins il y a des endroits qui sont francophones et anglophones.
   I intend to go and live in another country for a couple of years after my degree. I think that it is a good idea to go and to see how other people live. I would like to live in Canada. I can always visit the United States and at least there are places which are French-speaking and English-speaking.

5. **Que pensez vous de Facebook ?**
Facebook est un service de réseautage social en ligne sur Internet. Je pense que c'est une idée formidable mais il y a des dangers. Est-ce que vous savez que l'utilisateur cède à Facebook des droits de réutilisation sur toutes les données qu'il publie ? Je ne crois pas que ceci soit une bonne chose. J'utilise Facebook pour rester en contact avec des amis, mais je ne mets pas de photos ni de données trop personnelles.
Facebook is a social networking on-line site. I think that it is a great idea but there are dangers. Did you know that the user gives Facebook the right to re-use all information that he publishes? I don't believe that this is a good thing. I use Facebook to stay in contact with friends, but I don't put up photos or information which is too personal.

6. **La publicité est partout et très puissante. Que pensez-vous ?**
La publicité est omniprésente et on vit avec continuellement. C'est dans les journaux, à la télé, sur l'internet, sur les panneaux au bord de la route, enfin partout ! Je sais que pour les entreprises, la publicité est la seule façon de faire connaître leurs produits. Je ne suis ni pour ni contre la publicité. C'est parfois agaçant d'être confronté avec tant de publicité, surtout quand c'est de la publicité envahissante, mais je comprends que ce soit important pour les commerçants et les entreprises de se faire connaître.
Advertising is everywhere and we live with it continuously. It is in newspapers, on the TV, on the internet, on signs at the side of the road, really everywhere! I know that for businesses, advertising is the only way of making their products known. I am neither for nor against advertising. It is sometimes annoying to be faced with so much advertising, especially when it is in-your-face advertising, but I understand that it is important for traders and businesses to make themselves known.

7. **Est-ce que vous êtes pour ou contre la peine de mort ?**
Je suis complètement contre la peine de mort. Je trouve que c'est une pratique barbare. La vie est sacrée et la peine de mort ne réduit pas le taux de criminalité. Pour moi, c'est simple, la violence n'est pas une solution à la violence.
I am completely against the death penalty. I find that it is a barbaric practice. Life is sacred and the death penalty does not reduce the crime rate. For me, it is simple, violence is not a solution to violence.

Je suis pour la peine de mort à 100% (cent pour cent). Il y a ceux qui disent que la peine de mort ne réduit pas le taux de criminalité, mais ce dont on est sûr, c'est qu'elle ne le fait pas monter !
I am a 100% in favour of the death penalty. There are those that say that the death penalty does not reduce the crime rate, but one thing that we are sure of, it doesn't increase it!

8. **Le problème de la drogue est répandu en Irlande. Qu'est-ce qu'on peut faire pour limiter ses dégâts ?**
Il faut lancer des campagnes pour sensibiliser les jeunes. Je pense que l'éducation reste la clé. Il faut le répéter à maintes reprises ; la drogue est la voie certaine vers le vrai enfer. Je suis de l'avis que les peines doivent être plus sévères pour ceux qui revendent la drogue.
We must launch campaigns to inform young people. I think that education remains the key. It has to be repeated several times over; drugs are the surefire way to hell on earth. I am of the opinion that sentences should be more severe for those that deal drugs.

9. **Que feriez-vous pour améliorer le sort des immigrés clandestins ?**

   D'abord je pense que c'est important d'essayer de comprendre pourquoi ces gens sont venus chez nous. Pourquoi est-ce qu'ils ont pris des risques pour venir dans un pays où ils ne connaissent personne ? Il faut les traiter avec dignité et les écouter avec un esprit ouvert. On ne peut pas ouvrir les portes à tout le monde, mais il faut être perspicace.

   Firstly, I think that it is important to try and understand why these people have come to our country. Why have they taken risks to come to a country where they know no-one? They have to be treated with dignity and listened to with an open mind. We cannot open our doors to everyone, but we have to be discerning.

10. **Le crime est en augmentation dans nos villes en Irlande. Est-ce que le gouvernement fait assez pour lutter contre les gangs criminels ?**

    En dehors de Dublin, Limerick est vraiment connu pour ses gangs. La criminalité du pègre est bien documenté mais toujours d'une façon subjective. Les gens ne cherchent pas à savoir si la situation à Limerick est exagerée. Ici la violence est vraiment évidente mais dans certains quartiers seulement. Normalement les gens n'ont pas peur mais il faut être vigilant la nuit comme dans n'importe quelle autre grande ville. Les gangs constituent peut-être cinq ou six familles et la guerre reste entre eux. Le gouvernement ne fait pas assez pour protéger ses citoyens, mais c'est difficile, car il y a beaucoup de situations chancelantes à gérer en même temps. La police fait de son mieux mais elle est soumise aux contraintes budgétaires.

    Outside of Dublin, Limerick is really known for its gangs. Underworld criminality is well documented but always in a subjective way. People are not interested in knowing if the situation in Limerick is exagerated. Here violence is certainly evident but only in specific areas. Usually people are not afraid but you have to be careful at night like in any big city. The gangs are made up of maybe 5 or 6 families and the war stays between them. The government does not do enough to protect its citizens, but it is difficult, because there are a lot of delicate situations to manage at the same time. The police do their best but they are subjected to budgetary constraints.

Le Vocabulaire Essentiel

Français	Anglais	How to pronounce
émigrer	to emigrate	em-me-grey
la toxicomanie	drug abuse	la tox-ee-com-man-nee
se droguer	to take drugs	se drug-ay
un drogué	a drug addict	an drug-ay
un consommateur de drogue	a drug taker	an con-so-ma-tur de drug
un toxicomane	an addict	an tox-ee-com-man
être en manque	to crave drugs	etr on maunk
le pouvoir de dépendance	addictiveness	le poov-war de day-pon-donce

mourir d'un overdose	to die from an overdose	moo-rear dan over-dose
la désintoxication	detoxification	la days-an-tox-ee-cass-yon
désintoxiquer	to detoxify	days-an-tox-ee-kay
être sevré de	to be weaned off	etr sev-ray de
un centre de désintoxication	a drug clinic	an sont-re de days-an-tox-ee-cass-yon
la came	dope	la kam
les responsabilités sociales	social responsibilities	lay res-pon-sa-billy-tay so-see-al
des hallucinogènes	hallucinogens	days ah-lucy-oh-jen
se shooter avec	to get stoned on	se shoo-tay avek
un monde plus juste	a fairer world	an mond plu juste
plus équitable	more equal	plooz ek-key-tabl
des joueurs compulsifs	compulsive gamblers	day ju-er com-pul-seeve
le prix à payer	the price to pay	le pree-ah-pay-ay
un jeu de hasard	a game of chance	an juh de as-zar
pile ou face	heads or tails	peel oo fass
soumis à la chance	down to luck	sue-me ah la shonce
un tirage	a draw	an teer-raj
la distribution de cartes	the fall of the cards	la diss-tree-bweuce-yon
un jet de dé	a roll of the dice	an jay-de-day
quitter son pays	to leave one's country	key-tay son pay-ee
le droit à l'éducation	the right to education	le dwah ah led-you-cass-yon
la citoyenneté	citizenship	la sit-twy-ent-tay
la misère	poverty	la mee-zere
se réfugier	to take refuge	se re-fuj-ee-ay
le déplacement	displacement	le day-place-mon
fuir	to flee	fweer
la marijuana	marijuana	la maree-wana
l'herbe	weed	lerb
une meilleur vie	a better life	oone may-er vee
une minorité	a minority	oone me-nor-ree-tay
une ethnie	an ethnic group	oone et-nee
un raciste	a racist	an rah-cyst
antiraciste	non racist	an-tee rah-cyst
des émeutes raciales	race riots	days ay-mut rass-see-al
un conflit racial	a racial conflict	an con-flee rass-see-al
inciter à la haine raciale	to stir up racial hatred	an-seat-tay ah la en-rass-see-al

la discrimination raciale	*racial discrimination*	la diss-crim-min-ass-yon rass-see-al
une insulte raciale	*a racial slur*	oone an-soolt rass-see-al
un meurtre raciste	*a racial conflict*	an murt rah-cyst
être l'objet de discrimination	*to be discriminated against*	et-re lob-jay de diss-crim-min-nass-yon
souffrir de discrimination	*to endure discrimination*	soof-rear de diss-crim-min-ass-yon
travailler à plein temps	*to work full time*	tra-vye-ay ah plen-ton
à mi-temps	*part-time*	ah me-ton
le demandeur d'emploi	*a job-seekeer*	le duh-mon-dur dom-ploi
les chiffres du chômage	*unemployment figures*	lay sheaf-re do show-maje
baisser	*to drop*	bess-say
licencier	*to lay off, to make redundant*	lee-sawn-see-ay
embaucher	*to hire*	om-boh-shay
intérimaire	*temporary worker*	an-terry-mair
la consommation d'alcool	*alcohol consumption*	la con-so-mass-yon dal-cull
une étape incontournable	*an inevitable stage*	oone ay-tap an-con-tur-nabl
orner	*to embellish*	or-nay
la vie sociale	*social life*	la vee so-see-al
la rencontre avec l'alcool	*confronting alcohol*	la ron-contr avek lal-cull
les fêtes	*parties*	lay fett
les sorties	*nights out*	lay sor-tee
moins stigmatisé socialement	*less stigmatised socially*	mwan stig-ma-tee-zay so-see-al-mon
les producteurs d'alcool	*the alcohol producers*	lay pro-duck-tur dal-cull
la consommation très précoce	*under-age drinking*	le con-so-mass-yon tray pre-cuss
l'ivresse	*drunkenness*	leave-ress
un éthylotest	*a breathalyser*	an ay-tee-lo-test
l'alcool au volant	*drink driving*	lal-cull oh vuh-lon
une sous-classe	*an underclass*	oone sue-class
pauvre	*poor / destitute*	pauve
indigent	*indigent*	an-dee-jon
les défavorisés	*the underprivilged / the dispossessed / the have-nots*	lay de-fav-vor-ree-zay
les nécessiteux	*the needy*	lay ne-cess-see-teuh
les opprimés	*the downtrodden*	lays oh-preem-may
les rejetés de la société	*the throwaways*	lay re-jet-tay de la so-see-eh-tay

les déchets de la société	*the human dross*	lay de-shay de la so-see-eh-tay
la lie	*the scum*	la lee
les déchets	*the refuse*	lay de-shay
une épave	*a derelict*	oone ay-pav
un taudis	*a slum / a hovel*	an toe-dee
la zone	*skid row*	la zun
frappé par la pauvreté	*poverty-stricken*	frap-pay par la pauve-reh-tay
accablé par la pauvreté	*poverty-ridden*	ah-cab-blay par la pauve-reh-tay
seuil de pauvreté	*poverty line / poverty threshold*	soy de pauve-reh-tay
misère noire	*grinding poverty*	mee-zere nwar
pauvreté chronique	*entrenched poverty*	pauve-reh-tay cron-neek
joindre les deux bouts	*to make both ends meet*	jwand lay duh boo
grapiller une existence	*to eke out a living / to scrape a living*	grap-pee-ay oone eggs-zist-tonce
salaire de misère	*starvation wage*	sal-lair de mee-zere
être dans la gêne	*to be in poor circumstances / to be poorly off / to be badly off*	et don la jen
être fauché	*to be broke / to be hard up*	et foh-shay
ne plus avoir un sou	*to be penniless*	ne plooze av-war an sue
être sur la paille	*to be strapped*	et soor la pie
génétiquement identique	*genetically identical*	jen-nay-teek-mon mod-diffy-ay
un fragment d'ADN	*a fragment of DNA*	an frag-mon da-day-en
le bouturage	*propagation*	le boo-too-raje
un être vivant	*a living being*	an et vee-von
artificielle	*artificial*	ar-teh-fiss-see-el
les produits cosmétiques	*cosmetic products*	lay pro-dwee cos-meh-teek
la peau	*the skin*	la poh
torturer des animaux	*to torture animals*	tor-tur-ray days annie-moh
un débat	*a debate*	an de-bah
les testes scientifiques	*scientific tests*	lay test see-on-tiff-feak
une vie humaine	*a human life*	oone vee oo-men
les animaux cobayes	*animal guinea-pigs (testers)*	lay annie-moh co-bye
souffrir en silence	*to suffer in silence*	soof-rear on see-lonce

Chapitre 10 Les problèmes sociaux

Dix constructions clés sur les problèmes sociaux

1. **Autrement** = *otherwise*
   On doit aider les gens qui vivent dans les situations de précarité, autrement ils peuvent continuer sans espoir d'une vie meilleure.
   We must help people who live in precarious situations otherwise they can continue without the hope of a better life.

2. **Prendre en charge** = *to take responsibility for*
   C'est à nous tous de prendre en charge les enfants ravagés de la guerre.
   It is up to all of us to take responsibility for children ravaged by war.

3. **Il est nécessaire de** = *it is necessary to*
   Il est nécessaire de faire de son mieux pour subvenir aux besoins du peuple.
   It is necessary to do one's best to provide for the needs of the people.

4. **Grimper** = *to rise significantly*
   Le taux de chômage grimpe dans tous les pays occidentaux à la suite de la chute bancaire.
   The rate of unemployment is rising significantly in all western countries following the banking collapse.

5. **Cependant ceci** = *however this*
   La peine de mort est pratiquée dans plusieurs pays du Moyen Orient. Cependant ceci ne veut pas dire que ça soit juste.
   The death penalty is used in several middle eastern countries. However this is not to say that it is fair.

6. **Essentiellement** = *essentially, in essence*
   Le discours du Président français est essentiellement un aveu de culpabilité envers la population de la Chine.
   The French President's speech is essentially an admission of guilt toward the Chinese population.

7. **De plus en plus** = *more and more*
   Il y a de plus en plus de toxicomanes, mêmes dans les petits patelins.
   There are more and more drug addicts even in small villages.

8. **Tandis que** = *while*
   (This is a more formal way of saying while – most students will use pendant que)
   Le taux d'alcoolisme grimpe tandis que les entreprises qui fabriquent les boissons s'enrichissent.
   The level of alcoholism is rising significantly while the companies who manufacture drinks are getting richer.

9. **C'est particulierement difficile** = *it is particularly + adjective*
   C'est particulièrement difficile car les enfants ont besoin d'avoir des gens autour d'eux en qui ils puissent avoir confiance et sur qui ils puissent compter pour les conseiller et les aider à résoudre leurs problèmes.
   It is particularly difficult because children need to be surrounded by people that they can trust and that they can count on to advise them and help them solve their problems.

10. **C'est aussi une façon de + verb in the infinitive = *it is also a way of***
    C'est aussi une façon de dire que trop c'est trop !
    It is also a way of saying that enough is enough!

Dix expressions authentiques et ludiques

1. L'avocat du diable = *the devil's advocate* (someone who argues against a point in order to test its validity or to provoke debate)
2. Dormir comme un sabot = *to sleep very deeply*
3. Trancher le nœud gordien = *to cut the Gordian knot / to resolve a problem in an effective manner*
4. Tenir au courant / au jus = *to keep yourself informed*
5. Un cautère sur une jambe de bois = *a completely useless measure*
6. Dire pis que pendre = *to badmouth someone*
7. Se faire des cheveux (blancs) / du mouron / de la mousse = *to worry*
8. Un oiseau rare = *a person of exceptional qualities*
9. S'enfoncer tout seul = *to get into deeper trouble, to make matters worse for oneself*
10. Appuyer sur le champignon / conduire le champignon au plancher = *to accelerate / to drive with one's foot to the floor*

Acknowledgements

I would like to express my sincere thanks to everyone who assisted in the production of *Bonne Chance!* I would like to begin by thanking my husband Alan, for his practical advice and kindness, and my sons Michael and John for their patience. I would like to thank Charlotte for her spirit of motivation, which kept me going. Thank you also to my parents John and Maisie Hayes, and to my friends, Carmel Donnelly, Jennifer Larkin and Maria Gold for their continued support and advice. I would also like to thank my students in Colaiste Mhichil, Limerick. A special thank you to my 5th and 6th years, who used and commented on the material for *Bonne Chance!* Thanks lads. A very special thank you to all my colleagues, especially Ann Whelan, Suzanne Browne, Noelle Barry, Linda Donohoe, Jenny Harte and Elizabeth Quinn for their encouragement and invaluable insights. Finally, I would like to thank everyone at Gill & Macmillan, especially Aoileann O'Donnell, who made everything easier, and to Neil Ryan who kept me focused.

Merci Mille Fois.

Elizabeth Hayes-Lyne.